east coast rooms

east coa

Portfolios of 31
Interior Designers
and Architects

st rooms

Anna Kasabian

ROCKPORT PUBLISHERS

First published in the United States of America by
Rockport Publishers, Inc.
33 Commercial Street
Gloucester, Massachusetts 01930-5089
Telephone: (978) 282-9590
Facsimile: (978) 283-2742
www.rockpub.com

ISBN 1-56496-673-9

10 9 8 7 6 5 4 3 2 1

Cover Image: Design: Thomas O'Brien; Photography: Laura Resen,
courtesy of House Beautiful.

Book Layout: Sawyer Design Associates Inc.

Printed in China.

Dedicated to my late parents—my mother, Katie, who always dreamed dreams for me and my father, Dom, who gave me my writing genes—and my dear friend Cheryl Janecka who has been by my side with love and support since we met.

ACKNOWLEDGMENTS

First, my thanks to Martha Wetherill, my editor, who continues to have amazing grace and focused calm. This book, my second with her, has been pure joy to create. If she were a room, she would, as one designer put it, be "very Bali."

Thank you to all of the interior designers and architects for their wonderful contributions and insightful, honest, and entertaining looks behind the scenes at design—and themselves. We all will learn from this.

Very special thanks to the photographers whose talent and creativity will make these pages turn again and again. Your work makes this book happen. And, finally, thanks to Deborah Martin at *House Beautiful*, Linda LaChappelle, and Michael Strohl for your help.

contents

In my search to collect the most imaginative projects possible for inclusion in *East Coast Rooms,* I was quickly overwhelmed by the talent stream that runs from Maine to Washington, D.C. With that, I must say this book in no way pretends to represent the universe of designers and architects who have chosen to live on this part of the map.

An eclectic collection of rooms and their distinctive views, this book does represent a design truth shared by all within these pages: Rules are passé! Honesty is in! The message "do what is right for you" is a beacon burning bright, and that alone leads me to conclude that these are the best of design times.

The themes that run throughout this book all have to do with aligning rooms with comfort levels, with who the inhabitants are and how they want to use their space. Whether the designer created a city loft or a country bungalow, in each case furnishings, art, and building materials have come together more as an identity statement than as an expression of a particular design system.

It is particularly refreshing to see so many in the field with the confidence to place an eighteenth-century chair next to the satin sheen of a stainless-steel table, or to perch a hot-pink pillow on an antique chaise. The reasons vary from the desire to build rooms that showcase design sculptures from the past and present, to keeping a treasured family

heirloom in daily use, to the pleasure of finding the flea-market steal that just works. But beyond confidence, many people seem to have a genuine desire to ground their personal history in their rooms.

Several of the spaces featured are the homes of designers and architects themselves, and this freedom-to-be-me comes through loud and clear in their rooms. Common design threads include the use of natural fibers, particularly cotton and linen, and keeping backgrounds soothing and quiet so that art, sculpture, furniture, and accents in pillow fabric or carpeting can be fully appreciated without distraction.

Very often the designers and architects speak of the importance of light, whether natural or not, and how they work with it to create or enhance the moods and views they and their clients cherish.

Specifically, lots of attention is paid to outside light, which comes into play when choosing satin or flat wall coverings; deciding whether to ebonize, pickle or carpet floors; or whether to window dress with voluminous sheers or nothing at all.

Each and every detail counts as these artists paint a canvas of walls, windows, and rooms to fit the space and an individual or family lifestyle. With no rules to confine design, we all can move forward and create and live in rooms that revitalize, soothe, and inspire.

For designer William Sofield, this 1500-square-foot (135-square-meter) Fifth Avenue apartment—a McKim, Mead, and White building, no less—had a familiar list of problems to solve. (The views were not among them, by the way; the apartment looks out at the Empire State Building and beyond.) The design needed to be flexible enough to handle a crowd of one hundred for a Friday night party and still offer coziness and privacy for work-at-home days. The design challenge was further complicated by the fact that the space was being redesigned for a couple who would likely be moving to a larger space in a few years. Sofield thus had to assess furniture and other pieces for their flexibility for placement here and in an unspecified future home.

William Sofield

The living room and dining room functions coexist in one big room with ten-foot (three-meter) ceilings—a great feature when there's a crowd. To heighten the sense of space, the walls are painted taupe, gray, and white, beginning with the dark shades at the bottom and ending at the ceiling with the lightest. The furniture is spread around the room, keeping the core open and airy; a banquette couch can easily seat ten. The little bronze, glass-covered, cube-shaped table is purposefully set in front of the couch to treat guests to a reflection of the magnificent church just outside the window. For practicality, the couch arms are covered in leather while the seating is in a silk and cotton corduroy blend.

Traditional and contemporary furnishings are juxtaposed throughout. For example, the classic leather club chair—"the one Coco Chanel had in Paris"—is set steps from the ultra-contemporary sleek leather cab chairs. The warm, toasty tones, sheen, and curves work well together. In anticipation of the need for extra seating, two ottomans slip out of the way under the coffee table. When the couple wants to close off the living room and turn the teak dining room table into a desk, they slide the brushed-metal pocket door across the room. The buffet table is half filing cabinet, half buffet. Floors are old tiger oak in a charming herringbone pattern, and the marbling on the manteltop and on the coffee table are blends of the same colors.

The bedroom is "a salute to the super graphics of the 1970s." The beige-on-beige striped armoire behind the bed makes the point perfectly, as does the styling of the book-matched walnut bed. Notice how the stripe play on the walls is reversed to horizontal.

Lighting throughout the apartment is by lamp, to accentuate ceiling height. The exception is the foyer, where vintage 1970s spotlights replace lamps. Sofield was happy to add them to the scene. "I always love to incorporate things from people's past, especially if they're quirky. Objects like this have a history and add flavor."

(opposite) **The custom-made, teak-topped dining room table doubles as a desk; the glass top makes it easy to clean. Brushed-metal pocket doors slide across for privacy. To maintain visual interest, the silk curtains show as plaid when open, but turn into horizontal stripes when closed.**

(opposite) **One goal was to have a mix of contemporary and traditional furnishings that would infuse the room with rich design elements. Designer's luck led to a marble coffee table that perfectly matched the fireplace mantel. A soft beige Tibetan rug anchors this little entertainment island. Once pale and pickeled, the tiger oak floors were restored to their original chocolate tone.**

(above) **This comfortable banquette can seat ten people, but it is also a great place to sink into with a book, alone. The arms are covered with leather to save on wear and tear. Silk and cotton corduroy cover the seats and pillows.**

(right) **The bedroom salutes 1970s graphics with a stripe theme on the high-gloss enamel armoire that is reversed on the wall covering. In winter, the bedcover changes to a linen stripe as well. Warm tones are maintained throughout, a contrast to the cool light that comes from the north-facing windows.**

Photos: Andrew Bordwin

Charles Spada

Boston designer Charles Spada loves this tiny 600-square-foot (54-square-meter) space; it is one of his favorite apartments in the city. Perched on top of what was once a Baptist church in the South End, it is, in Spada's words, like a little Parisian hideaway carved out of the roof. Invisible at street level, once inside it reveals dramatic views of the city, especially from the patio. The design challenge was clear from the start: to help create the perfect background for an art collection of eighteenth- and nineteenth-century German, Italian, and French drawings and sepia landscapes. These personal treasures came from the owners' world travels, and include gouaches, watercolors, and charcoals.

Crown moldings were removed to keep the rooms simple and clean; this space, after all, was not about the architecture, but about art. Next, the walls, ceiling, and woodwork were all painted art-gallery white. The very dark, walnut parquet flooring makes the furniture feel as though it is floating. All of the furniture, which has a neo-classical mood, was made to order and scaled for the space. For example, the living room couch is tailor made to stretch across an entire wall; no end tables confine the seating scheme. The fluted wooden base and limestone top of the dining room table fit the mood, as does the Empire

(left) **The dark parquet floor helps give the impression that the furniture—much of it customized for the space—is floating. The main design goal of giving the owners' art collection a suitable, clean background was accomplished by removing architectural details like crown moldings and painting the walls art-gallery white.**

candelabra and peeling wrought-iron garden urn. The quintessential nineteenth-century lantern over the table keeps old Boston in the dinner view.

To hide the air conditioner, without detracting from the decor or inhibiting air flow, Spada custom designed a screen—made by stretching deer fencing, an inexpensive burlap material, across a frame. Art was strategically placed where the light was right for the colors, details, scene, or portrait. Designer Roger Lussier, whose expertise helped coordinate the look, handled the framing. Many fabrics are

(above) **The dining room table-for-two works perfectly in this space. Bostonians will recognize the lantern, which resembles city streetlamps. The table's column-shaped base is wood and the top a silky-smooth limestone. The theme is carried over to a storage console made from an enormous column; its shelves work well for both linens and glassware. A baker's table, tucked against the wall, can be used as a server for dinner parties.**

(right) **This art wall seemed to call for a long shelf—the perfect setting for a select grouping of tasteful art pieces. The lamps balance the look and, in the evening, they softly light the art above.**

soft Scalamandre chenille in earthy tones or white, which makes items recede rather than jump out. The design intent is for the eye to travel calmly and peacefully around the room.

The penthouse opens to a terrace from which Spada let the light pour in by using only filtering white sheers hung on brass swing rods for drapes. This minimal treatment also reduces the visual separation of inside and out. Artist Cheryl Battaglia added a magical touch—a soft pattern of stones—to the Spada-designed bedside tables and other furniture. In the end, the designer achieved his goal without compromise, and created a light-filled, elegant art sanctuary.

(right) **A French carpet in burnt butterscotch with a low pile and tight weave keeps the bedroom quiet and cozy. The sand-colored headboard is one of Spada's special designs. It is contoured to be comfortable when your back is against it, tapering from the top down to the mattress. The little side tables are a Spada design as well, but Boston artist Cheryl Battaglia worked in the sub-tle stone pattern on the surface and legs. The one fabric here is a silk-linen combination.**

Photos: Eric Roth

a penthouse makeover

Originally a hat factory, which was later transformed into a Woodstock-style, hot-tub and disco extravaganza, this 40- by 80-foot (12- by 24-meter) penthouse was space

Shelton Mindel and Reed Morrison

that needed a visionary. Architects Lee Mindel, Peter Shelton, and Reed Morrison looked beyond the centrally-placed, black fiberglass hot tub, an exclamation point for the past owner, to the raw potential of the space. The challenge was to integrate the space into the city via open vistas and to display a twentieth-century collection of furniture and decorative arts. Here was a space, if there were windows on all four sides, with take-your-breath-away views of the Empire State Building, Chrysler Building, the East and Hudson rivers, all from the twelfth floor. And, here was a space that, if built out properly, could be manipulated to open and close off rooms and views depending on the day or the activity.

A distinctive feature of the neighborhood is the presence of water tanks, whose forms ultimately inspired those of the sculpted, geometric interior lit from a rotunda and a glass cage rising through the ceiling. The rotunda is graced with exposure to the sky, access to the roof, and an open, airy gallery. A double-helix, stainless-steel and concrete staircase moves gracefully through the space.

(right) **This view of the living room emphasizes the dramatic and diverse views of the penthouse and demonstrates how sunny it can get. The milk-white walls and warm, honey-toned wood floor are the perfect backdrop to display the furniture collection.**

A sitting room hideaway, "part water tower, periscope, and observation tower," is at the roof level. About 40 windows were installed to take advantage of the four exposures and the rooftop level, and to fulfill the goal of bringing the cityscape inside. The windows are clean blocks of glass that keep the view pure and focused.

Public and private spaces are separated by an L-shaped service bar with two layers of floor-to-ceiling sliding panels; in fact, combinations of panels are found throughout the space. The service bar contains the bathrooms, storage, washer, dryer, and kitchen. Besides the panels, the aggregate quartz concrete floor also maps this section. A simple palette of plaster, stainless steel, wood, and white structural glass brings all architecture and art details into easy focus. The creations of Jean Prouvé, Charles Eames, Alexander Calder, Robert Ryman, Jacob Jacobsen, Josef Hoffman, and others are thoughtfully positioned throughout.

(opposite) **Simple, elegant, and filled with light, the space is serene, allowing the owner's extensive art and furniture collection to shine through.**

(above) **This peek into the dining room highlights the diverse architectural details and illustrates the unusual creative flair that went into the design of this visual pleasure dome. Joseph Hoffman chairs work their way around the table—a Shelton Mindel creation—beneath the light of a Venini chandelier, once commissioned by Syrie Maugham for Lord Mountbatten.**

(following pages) **A wall of golden anegre wood backs a simple bed and warms the room, which lacks natural light. Where city views and light are the focus in other rooms, here the beauty of this single architectural detail is paramount.**

Photos: Michael Moran

Jeffrey Bilhuber

Designer Jeffrey Bilhuber has been editing the design of this Coopersburg, Pennsylvania, home for the past fifteen years, and it continues to be one of his most rewarding and fulfilling. He says, "It challenges my perception of what is modern today; the foundation has not changed, and that is the critical benchmark."

Work began on this 1920s home during "times when all excess was acceptable." Bilhuber instead opted for a soft palette of neutrals. This approach was daring for the mid-1980s, when heavily saturated colors of indigo, garnet, and emerald green were common. Natural light freely plays off the walls and floors, and deep, dark shadows not only mark the passage of time, but also set off shapes within the space. Labeled minimalist then, the design today can be called "essentialism—what you need to fill your days with beauty."

The whole, rather than its parts, is what stands out in this home. The house features pieces from the sixteenth century to the twentieth, from the drafting table belonging to Gustave Eiffel (perhaps used when he designed the Eiffel Tower) to L.L. Bean canoe chairs on the porch. Calling this approach eclectic would be incorrect because

(left) **Sitting at Bilhuber's low, slatted-wood table on L.L. Bean canoe chairs unites one with the landscape as cool breezes move through the space. The magnificent view of "grass rivers," the creation of landscape architect A.E. Bye, mimics the undulations of the distant blue mountain ridge. The light and shadows that emphasize these design elements join the light play on the walls and floors inside.**

the technique focuses on the match rather than the mix—and the match must be seamless to work. For example, the works of art in the dining room, fern prints from the 1860s, are full scale and hung glass on glass. The heavier ferns are placed on the bottom of the walls and the lighter, more fluid ones are hung on a higher plane—the goal being to fill the room with energy. The unusual, delicate wood table came from the famous Kiluna Farms on Long Island, owned by Babe and Bill Haley, former president of CBS. The sideboard is an eighteenth-century French piece and the chairs are Directoire, slipcovered for summer. When winter arrives, the slipcovers come off and the rugs return to reveal a tawnier palette.

For the living room walls, Bilhuber chose to use squares of bark which change tone with the time of day. A great addition to an already visually compelling room is Sven Lukin's jumping frogs, mounted on tarpaper and set right on the wall sans frames. Frames would have been a visual disruption to the energy of the "free" jumping frogs.

(right) **A stunning 1920s black-and-white marble floor sets a casual mood in this book-filled sunroom. Bilhuber built the dramatic scorched bamboo and lacquered bookcases and chose a very unusual split-reed wall covering to add to the warmth of the space.**

(above) **Squares of bark paper, originally designed by Bilhuber for use in an art gallery, cover the living room walls and set off the jumping frog art of Sven Lukin, which is set on squares of black tarpaper. Deciding not to frame the frogs set them free to move over the walls. A black floor dramatizes the white funiture.**

(opposite) **The palette of this country retreat comprises a huge array of neutrals punctuated by ebony and mahogany—all woven seamlessly with design elements that mix past and present. A perfect example is this breathtaking dining room, with its simple and elegant decor set off by the dominant crisp, chilled shades of white. Called "Nature-Printed Ferns," the 1860s art presents a visual balance but is in no particular order, conveying a pleasing energy and rhythm of green.**

When Celeste Cooper designed her home in Boston's luxury low-rise, the Four Seasons, she chose not conform to expected design dynamics. The designer worked instead to

Celeste Cooper

create space that honestly reflects both the architecture of this twentieth-century building and her own rebellious persona. There isn't a hint of a Martha Stewart palette or Ralph Lauren here, nor the fantasy of a country room or English cottage. "The mandate of interior designers is to have the architecture tell you what to do," she says.

Spare in style, the fabrics, materials, and decor choices represent the designer's rigorously self-indulgent exercise. The Miesian box was stripped to bare walls and the space reapportioned in a way that emphasizes shapes rather than ornamentation. Minimalism is a most appealing goal, but it is difficult to attain in the midst of busy lives, with all the accompanying impedimenta—office equipment, pots and pans, books, magazines, and so on. To solve the problem, copious closed-door storage was designed to obscure the "stuff" of life.

For designers, as for clients, the home is a sanctuary. These rooms were created to house a peaceful domain, from the striking, cool, clean-lined kitchen to the master bath of concrete and stainless steel. Nothing is added to distract attention from the shapes of the rooms. The built-ins, furniture, and materials—smooth, sleek, reflective, cool—draw one in to an appreciative focus. The kitchen features an unusual combination of black wood cabinets (sprayed with an industrial finish), stainless-steel countertops and backsplash, and a black rubber Pirelli floor. The stainless steel continues with insets in the concrete floor of the master bath; this is a nice touch, as is the mirroring on the cabinets.

What is striking in these rooms is that the simplicity of the materials creates a serene atmosphere. The living room expresses this theme with a fireplace dressed simply with a plain slab of granite. "The idea was to treat the fireplace in an iconoclastic manner; it didn't need a mantel, precious stone hearth, or picture hanging over it," Cooper says. The couch, done in a simple, comfortable chenille, wraps around two sides of this 20- by 30-foot (6- by 9-meter) room and seats twenty-five.

The two large, ebonized-ash coffee tables are often used for dining. Space, Cooper says, is a precious commodity, and to devote an entire room to the imagined ceremony of family meals is "another folly of not living the way we live." In fact, she often turns dining rooms into libraries, if clients are willing. There is no art on the walls because the architecture itself is art. The philosophy expressed in this home is all about truth in living and truth in design.

(opposite) **A big, comfortable chenille couch wraps around two sides of this 20- by 30- foot (6- by 9-meter) living room and can seat up to twenty-five guests. Two ebonized-ash coffee tables hold drinks or dinner.**

(right) **Architecture is art in itself for Celeste Cooper, who emphatically rejects the idea of using art as decoration. Therefore, the walls are bare and the fireplace is adorned with neither mantel nor "precious" stone hearth; the focus is on the simple beauty of this part of the space.**

(above) **Stainless steel, mirrored glass, and concrete make this master bath rich with texture and the play of light. The stainless steel seems to glow and float above the cabinetry while the concrete floor provides a pleasing textural contrast and design anchor.**

(opposite) **The black wood and stainless steel emphasize the clean lines of this kitchen and maintain the desired minimalist feel. The black Pirelli rubber floor was chosen for its texture, comfort, and visual appeal.**

Photos: Richard Mandelkorn

engaging contrasts

When interior designer Albert Hadley moved into this classic 1920s apartment on the upper east side of Manhattan, he wanted to create a living space "as simple and

Parish Hadley

unpretentious as possible." To accomplish this, the background of the space is clean and painted in a creamy white. The living room walls are made to seem as though they are floating; they are edged in recessed mirror and the wood floor ebonized to emphasize the liftoff. Fabrics, furnishings, art, and sculpture provide plenty to look at and, being well placed, allow every item to be studied for detail and craftsmanship.

Hadley's staff says he often demonstrates a "continuity in the madness," a phrase that summarizes this city nest. The living room houses a fainting couch that once belonged to his grandfather; it is capped with a 1920s silk quilt and sits next to a cowhide rug. A small red table breaks up the shades of cream like a little design siren; it features a bronze pull made by Connecticut sculptor Mark Sciarrillo. The couch with the tufted back made its way here from Hadley's country house. Nearby is an interesting old German bookcase that steps up like a pyramid. The contrasts in periods, design, and materials are quite engaging.

The apartment does not really have a dining room. A table and chairs are placed in a room that looks like a dining room, but the designer emphasizes that it is used rather as a sitting room and library. The pretty, robin's-egg blue wall with art—including a 1929 painting of decorator Elsie DeWolf—doubles as a bulletin board; it is made of cork with gilded molding. Two bronze diving boy sculptures from the 1950s are set on silver-leaf bases—they look like they are tumbling into warm Caribbean waters. The dark wood chairs surrounding the table are German and covered in a high-sheen, rough silk. The berry-red chairs are shown here, but others are covered in M&M blue and yellow "to keep the look fresh and interesting."

The views are interesting no matter which way one turns. Through the doorway to the bathroom, a little window is framed with a collage of pieces including a gilded wood table with a marble top and a zebra-patterned hooked rug. Everywhere there is something to catch the eye from the floor up, and everything has a distinctive shape, color, and texture.

(opposite) **A big, robin's-egg blue cork bulletin board breaks up the repetitive patterned wallpaper with a splash of color, allows for a quick change in art, and provides a place for tasks to be noted with flair. This room is used as a library and sitting room. To change the mood, Hadley lights the candle in the Italian hurricane globe.**

(following pages) **To make the walls seem as if they are floating, the floors are ebonized and the ceiling edged in mirror. The walls are a creamy white; little splashes of color are introduced via art, furnishings, and an old silk quilt.**

(right) **A bold little zebra rug draws the eye into the master bath entry, where a jumble of design elements and styles—from a gilded wood table to a sea-green glass ball sculpture—sit on the same plane in harmony. This design snapshot summarizes Hadley's style.**

(opposite) **An old German bookcase with painted inlays and scenes of athletic events sits like a grand wooden pyramid against a milky white wall. It is one of many out-of-the-ordinary pieces that are woven through the space, catching the eye and often bringing a smile.**

Photos: Pieter Estersohn

a home for gathering and retreat

Thomas O'Brien's search for the perfect apartment—dramatic space good both for entertaining andretreat—ended during his tour of this space in a Manhattan high-rise.

Thomas O'Brien

Eighteen-foot (5.5-meter) ceilings and huge casement windows in the living room infused the place with light and drama; it was easy to envision a party in full swing. With engaging views from the seventeenth floor and a terrace that felt "very New York," the apartment would just as easily make a quiet retreat from the busy world of work.

The next step was to personalize the space. The walls were painted with the designer's favorite grayish-white Pratt and Lambert Timidity, which looks great during the day and takes on a pleasing hue in the evening. The rest of the palette is bone, beige, and buttery tones. The floor is white—a refreshing change from the ebony floor of O'Brien's office—and takes on a luminous character at night. The cluster of seating, a variety of styles, and the mix of fabric and leather are anchored by the marble and wood fireplace. The design of the simple, clean mantle shelf is based on one O'Brien saw in his travels; the goal was a "strong, simple silhouette."

Visual interest is raised through the different materials of the pillows and throws and through furnishings with dramatic contrasts, like the chocolate walnut-wood–topped tables on polished aluminum bases. O'Brien's favorite theme of chocolate against light caramel—the "saddle-shoe effect"—creates strong, simple design silhouettes in space. The limited color palette is complemented by a variety of fabric textures, including Italian linen, silk file, and tiger velvet from Brunswick and Fee. Furnishings for the apartment were a wonderful mix of old possessions and new finds from varying locales. They include Venezuelan cowhides; a mahogany armoire rescued from an outdoor market, which is used to hold guests' coats; and the designer's old chairs, which were revived for this space. A 1940s Chinese modern cabinet, once a yellow tone, was lightened and put to creative use—it conceals a television and other stored items.

(opposite) **A mix of nineteenth-century continental and English-style chairs complement the walnut tops and polished aluminum bases of the tables. Two tables can be pulled together to make a large buffet for entertaining. The chairs were in "a wonderful state of disrepair" before coming here. They are upholstered in Collobrieres fabric from Pierre Frey of Paris. The mahogany armoire was rescued from an outdoor market. It is used to holdr guests' coats.**

(right) **Huge windows let in lots of light and create a dramatic atmosphere for designer Thomas O'Brien's seventeenth-floor, Manhattan living room. The interest level of the limited, seamless palette of white, beige, bone, and bleached woods is raised with the integration of interesting fabrics, from nubby-Italian-linen–covered chairs to tiger velvet pillows. The 1940s Chinese modern cabinet, once a yellow tone, was lightened; it conceals a television and other stored items.**

(following pages) **This view of the living room demonstrates the designer's preference for contrasting shades of chocolate against lighter tones of beige and bone. Notice the Venezuelan cowhide rugs—a tough find—which look like clouds over the light wood floor.**

to the beach house

When in Manhattan, designer Vicente Wolf escapes to an austere, minimalist loft filled with pieces collected from his world travels. When the weekend comes, if he's not in Thailand, New Zealand, or the French countryside, he travels to his

Vicente Wolf

beach house on the very tip of Long Island. For Wolf, the beach house is both a great influence on his work and the place where he relaxes, entertains, and gardens.

Set one hundred feet (30 meters) above the ocean, the house has seamless views across the garden to the sea. Wolf purchased the beach house eighteen years ago and takes delight in its constantly evolving design. Although the look always appears cohesive, the home's contents are "guests" invited from yard sales and auctions as well as from around-the-world travels. The charming drop-leaf table came from a yard sale, the traditional side chair was obtained through an auction coup, and the beach-themed photographs collected from hither and yon.

Wolf's design equation combines form, function, and convenience. The kitchen, for example, is about function; glass doors on the refrigerator and exposed shelves reveal their contents. The all-white furniture theme is meant to enhance the ocean view rather than compete with it. Color is introduced via the pillow fabrics and little details, such as the

(right) **The all-white living room furniture and pale sea-green pillows keep the mood casual and elegant while allowing the ocean views to dominate. In the winter, the white slipcovers are lifted to reveal a taupe wool that instills a cozy feeling while maintaining the clean look.**

dartwork on the pillows, and that color is as pale as can be—a dreamy shade of blue green that looks like seawater. The same fabric sweeps over and softens the look of the dining room table. In the winter, the slipcovers come off to reveal an upholstered taupe wool that's warm and easy to sink into.

The floors are of crab orchard slate, which is more commonly used on exterior walls. Its natural tones work well in the house; it is laid like a pathway through a garden to the master bedroom, where a snow-white, overstuffed sleigh bed and a massive eighteenth-century mirror steal the view. Steps from the bed, in the master bath, is a nineteenth-century French copper soaking tub with a glow that lights the room.

The dining room, living room, and kitchen all face the ocean, with spectacular views. Overnight guests stay in the guest room, carpeted for quiet in cut heather wool in a shade of wet sand. Like the rest of the house, the guest room graces a light, airy mood with voile curtains swinging in the ocean breeze. The guest bed is made of upholstered mattresses, so that what functions as a couch with toss pillows by day instantly transforms into a comfortable sleeping area at night.

(above) **The clean, white lines are continued through the kitchen and the simple, yet cozy dining nook.**

(opposite) **The guest bedroom makes a perfect retreat with quiet colors, plenty of books, and a comfortable couch that transforms into a bed when needed.**

(following pages) **The sleigh bed in the master bedroom upholds the white theme, while anchoring the room. The huge, eighteenth-century mirror serves to open the space.**

Photos: Vicente Wolf

Looking at this cool, serene, ultra-clean apartment in Boston's Harbor Towers, it is hard to imagine that seventeen floors below is the tangle of construction that is

Peter Forbes

Boston's infamous Big Dig and the unsettling din that is now normal to the neighborhood. This space is a statement—about views, comfort, serviceability and beauty—for architect Peter Forbes, who designed it for his family. The original layout, a mix of wasted space and poorly sized rooms, was a maze that had to be dismantled in order to make way for this skybound retreat. Additional goals were improved lighting and storage.

The strength of this I.M. Pei building is its views. The Forbes unit faces the stuff of postcards: Boston Harbor, the North End, Faneuil Hall, the State House, and the Customs Tower. Night and day, these scenes are captivating. The choppy layout of the rooms broke up the views, so the interior walls were eliminated.

However, an open layout presents privacy issues. Forbes found solutions such as a curved frosted-glass wall partition that shields the master bedroom. Both reflective and luminescent, the glass wall gathers and distributes light throughout the apartment. And, passages behind the glass screen to the kitchen are specifically dimensioned to accommodate only the family cat!

(left) The "everything table" and sometime dining room table was originally a prototype designed for a client. It is lit by an Achille Castigleone classic, which is from the 1960s.

Urban dwellings are often places where serenity is particularly sought. The last thing this family wanted to see was
the clutter of daily life, so intelligent storage areas were
designed to disappear. The perimeter of the space is lined
with nine closets, cupboards, and a study carrel, all con-
cealed behind hinged wooden panels. The kitchen is a
"functional cube" that also contains closets and
cupboards. To continue the visual calm, all the architectural
trims were removed and the doorways cleared to the
ceiling. The clarity of the spaces allows attention to focus
on the objects within them.

In keeping with the clean theme, furnishing is minimal and
neutral or white. The raw, tough-as-nails linen fabric on the
sofas came from Italy and survived the rigors of both cat
and baby play. The side chairs are a simple canvas. The
dining room table is really an "everything table" for the family. Perimeter walls are painted white and the core is
unpainted plaster, which has a bit of shine and depth.

The flooring is the same shiny black marble that typifies a
commercial bank's decor, but the look was transformed
with sandblasting. The color changed to a blue-gray hue
and the new texture feels like cool suede—particularly
pleasant on bare feet.

(right) **The pristine, stainless-steel kitchen, a "functional cube," is in keeping
with the clean, cool, serene mood throughout.**

(above) **This curved, frosted-glass screen provides privacy for the bedroom. Being American glass, it has a hint of green in the reflection; European glass, made of a different silicon sand, gives off a gray light. A sheet of plastic incorporated in the middle of the glass obscures fingerprints.**

(opposite) **Simple, functional, and sturdy furnishings complete the living room. An Italian factory made the sofas and covered them in a tough raw linen to survive the play of both cat and baby. Simple canvas chairs border the coffee table. Toio lamps from the 1960s are made with real automobile headlights that adjust up and down. High beams shoot out at the walls and dazzle party guests, while the low beams come on at dusk on normal days.**

Photos: Nick Wheeler, © Wheeler Photographics

Manhattan designer Thomas Jayne is known for dovetailing the historic with the contemporary, and for enriching rooms with vibrant colors. This apartment, of which he was

Thomas Jayne

both decorator and resident, demonstrates that he can practice what he preaches.

Jayne also, on occasion, likes to interject a little humor in his design schemes. Take, for example, the design collage he created in a little slice of his apartment where an antique mezzotint of a bustled lady with her romping pup sits above a Persian rug floating atop checkerboard tiles. Add to the scene a one-of-a-kind sculpted mirror with details that resemble tree branches, and it all fits together in a way that brings a smile to a guest's face. In explaining his discovery and subsequent re-design of the space, Jayne noted that it was like many design projects one after the other—a caterpillar-to-butterfly design evolution. It was functional and had a good basic layout, but it needed a decorator's vision to really fly.

At first glance, Jayne noted the space was defined only by its white walls and carpeted floors—neither of which made the space very interesting. But once Jayne began to work

(left) **Jayne created a rich roomscape of color, texture, patterns, and fabrics and, like a wise tailor, seamlessly wove the old with the new. The eye moves smoothly around the room, from the pristine, ruddy brown cork floor to the bordering books, antique desk, and all the little design details.**

with the space, he uncovered hidden character and details he could utilize in his final design. For example, beneath the carpet was a gem of a floor—original cork, it dated back to the 1920s. The unveiling left Jayne quite pleased.

The white walls, too flat for the designer's taste, were immediately altered. First he painted stripes to liven up the look and add a bit of color. But, as time passed and new pieces of art and furniture—a mix of antiques and new pieces—were introduced, the striped walls no longer worked. It was then that he decided to glaze over the stripes and stencil them with a humorous oversized paisley reminiscent of a familiar nineteenth-century pattern.

In furnishing the apartment, Jayne wove auction and antique store finds throughout the apartment, and sat them next to select, treasured family pieces. For example, the big, dark, wood desk, circa 1870, is a cherished piece from Jayne's grandparents' home. Likewise, the centerpiece of his bedroom is a beautiful dark wood Victorian bed that once belonged to his great-grandparents. An ornate headboard climbs the wall and sets somewhat

(right) **The centerpiece of the bedroom is the beautiful dark wood Victorian bed, which once belonged to the designer's great-grandparents. The ornate headboard climbs the wall and sets a regal tone. Simple built-in bookshelves flank the bed and are painted to match the wall so as not to stop the eye.**

Photos: Andrew Garn

of a regal mood. Simple, built-in bookshelves flank the bed but remain in the background as they are painted to match the wall. Deep moss-green silk curtains maintain the regal feeling, and balance the theme that integrates old and new. Custom made in London by Claremont, they are hung on antique metal rings. Windows overlooking uninspiring views are shielded with blinds.

The dining table centerpiece, an eighteenth-century server atop a new, mirrored tray, is, to Jayne, a metaphor for the entire apartment, where old and new live harmoniously. The two lamps beside the buffet have special meaning; they come from Jayne's former employer, the famous decorator Kevin McNamera.

(left) **The dining table and buffet are located on the far side of the living room. The centerpiece, an eighteenth-century server atop a new mirrored tray, is, to Jayne, "a metaphor for the apartment," where old and new live harmoniously. The two lamps beside the buffet have special meaning, as they come from Jayne's former employer, the famous decorator Kevin McNamera.**

(below) **This wonderful little corner of Jayne's apartment features a rich slice of his design composition. The humorous antique mezzotint of the bustled lady with her romping pup, the Persian rug floating atop checkerboard tiles, and the sculpted mirror that resembles branches all come together in a pleasing plane.**

Photos: Andrew Garn

designs for a partnership

Dakota Jackson

Originally created for a Showhouse, this highly personalized sanctuary by Dakota Jackson reveals the life he shares with his wife, art historian and cultural critic RoseLee Goldberg, in their Manhattan home. The books, musical instruments, simultaneously running Gilbert & George and Laurie Anderson videos, the partners' desk, art, and furniture are like the threads of the silken web that is this couple's relationship. Their shared interest in design and architecture is apparent in the Buckminster Fuller book collection.

The walls of the room are punctuated with art by peers and friends including Cindy Sherman, Robert Longo, Lou Reed, and Vincent Desiderio. The family photographs are by Arthur Elgort. In homage to his design influences, Jackson assembled a collection of classic furniture from renowned designers Pierre Chareau, Eugene Printz, Marcel Breuer, and Frank Lloyd Wright, as well as architectural models from Eisenman Architects. A group of rare string and percussion instruments adds to the room's personality.

This room has no windows, which perpetuates the illusion of time uninterrupted by daylight, dusk, or weather. Without walls, the room is divided into zones for sitting, viewing, and other activities. One visual divide appears where a section of the walls is made of highly reflective Venetian plaster with an overlay grid in black and red pencil inspired by painter Agnes Martin. Another section is created by a series of translucent, architectonic screens that obscure the windows.

This is a place where the couple conducts research, shares ideas, reads, and plays music. The partners' desk is a perfect place for easy conversation, but it is also emblematic of the shared course of this couple's lives over many years. Jackson says this room could appear exorbitant and exclusive to the casual observer; that was not his intention, however. His goal was to combine the various rooms people live in most into one room.

(opposite) **The room encompasses various activity zones, this being the reading corner where the couple's Buckminster Fuller book collection lives. A clean-lined, snugly upholstered, butter-yellow chair is set under a light angled perfectly for reading.**

(following pages) **Central to the theme is the couple's partners' desk, set on an island of rug surrounded by 16- by 32-inch (40- by 80-cm) panels of deep brown birch plywood. This is where the designer and his wife share ideas and converse about the day.**

(above) The windows were purposely obscured here; a visual divide was created with wall treatments. The Venetian plaster refers to the paintings of Agnes Martin; it creates an illusion of depth, enhancing the surface and tactile quality of the wall. The other section is distinguished by a series of translucent, architectonic screens. Illuminated from behind by artificial light, this glowing surface contains visual interest within the interior of the room.

(right) A group of rare string and percussion instruments, Jackson's piano, family portraits by Arthur Elgort, and the art of friends and peers provide inspiration and encourage thought.

Photos: © Bill Geddes, 1999

It had been several years since interior designer Lynn Morgan's friend called on her to help with a palette makeover at her riverfront Victorian. The owner of the 1886 Connecticut home wanted to move far away from the bright periwinkle and chartreuse with salmon accents that had led the palette. She wanted Morgan to help quiet the color, calm the mood, and, ultimately, provide a better backdrop for her art and collections.

Lynn Morgan Design

Another goal was to make the house more livable for the family. That meant new fabrics, wall and floor coverings, and revised seating arrangements. The tall rooms with big windows were already the perfect setting to showcase her collections. The designer's role was strictly as a colorist and advisor on fabrics and, more broadly, to endorse her friend's inherently fine eye and good ideas.

Furnishings, a mix of antiques and family heirlooms, were re-covered in a calming shade of pale green cotton and accented with pillows in pale blue. Nothing was tossed from the mix, just refreshed and, in some cases, rearranged to encourage use. For example, the couch sitting in the bay window in the living room, which was given to the owner when she graduated from college, has a classic shape that does not go out of style, so it was retained. It works perfectly in the room, setting off the deep, rich wood coffee table. The coffee table was originally a bed; the owner saw its potential as a table and had it cut down to a size that worked in the space.

To keep maintenance down and to accommodate the traffic and spills that come with having children in the house, sturdy sea-grass carpeting was chosen for the floors in the living room and dining room. In the latter, the sea grass runs from wall to wall and is glued right to the floor. It is easy to vacuum and not even tomato juice will sink in and stain.

The 150-year-old wooden dining room table can accommodate twelve diners and is encircled with antique chairs in a variety of styles. A delicate shade of blue is introduced via the collection of Chinese export porcelain pots that trail from the tabletop to the mantel, where they are filled with tight clusters of deep green dried flowers.

To keep the open, airy feeling and to allow the natural light to illuminate the art, the windows are all free of drapes. Just outside the dining room is the front hallway, where heavy traffic took a toll on the wood floor. The solution was to paint it with big squares, which also added visual interest to this pivotal area.

(opposite) **By keeping the walls pale and set back, the art and collections take the limelight. Here we see the high detail of Sheffield candlesticks, children's chairs, and mixed media work by Lois Lane.**

(following pages, left) **High ceilings and a sunny bay window provide the perfect backdrop so furnishings and design accents can take center stage.**

(following pages, right) **The warm brown wood tones and harvest-yellow grass rug are set off by the delicate blue of this porcelain collection. A Susan Rothenberg painting breaks up the expanse of the sea-green wall above the mantel.**

(opposite) **The idea was to make the bedrooms as calm and peaceful as possible. The walls are pale pastels, furnishings are held to bare necessities, and the absence of draperies keeps the look open and airy.**

(above, top) **A postcard river view is framed in the doorway of this 1886 Victorian family home in Connecticut.**

(above, bottom) **Wooden rockers line this pristine, wide wooden porch, ready for family members to come sip afternoon tea or cozy up with a great novel. The clean design foreshadows the interior.**

When interior designer Christopher Coleman was designing his Chelsea apartment, he had a few special requirements. First, this being a rental property, he wanted to

Christopher Coleman

keep his budget in
check. And because
he was rarely home to enjoy the daylight, he wanted to
create a pleasant color scheme that would envelope him
when he came home in the evenings. Finally, he wanted to
create a clean design aesthetic which would provide an
appropriate background to best display his collection of
American paintings.

He opted for painting the walls a warm ochre so that
evening lamplight would produce a pleasant glow. To dress
up the walls and provide added visual interest, he
hammered in a double row of brass upholstery nails a few
inches below the ceiling. For the cost of just a few
packages of upholstery nails, he added a distinctive touch
to the walls in this 15- by 24-foot (4.6- by 7.3-meter) living/
dining room.

His flea market treasures from various periods, and the
contrasts of light and dark woods, make the scene rich with
detail and color. Conversation pieces accumulated over
time—a wonderful old French daybed, a lamp perched atop
an authentic camera tripod, custom side tables accented
with old radiator covers—all add to the room's interest.
Coleman created other imaginative devices, like the long,

shallow—sixteen-inch (40-cm)—linen-skirted table in the
passage to the office that conveniently hides storage boxes.

The big, flowing curtains in various doorways are a modern
version of the portieres used in the Victorian period to stop
doorway drafts. They add color, texture and a bit of
romance to the room. Some feature two-sided fabric
panels which change with the seasons. In winter, or cold
gloomy months, he shows the dark orange. In spring and
summer, the side with a lighter hue is in full view. To break
up the expected, one of the doors is hung with a one-of-a-
kind, brightly-colored, Indian-patterned fabric portiere.

It was important to Coleman to give his guests a choice of
seats, and the option of personalizing the seating arrangements. Among the choices are ornate Egyptian chairs that
are inlaid with mother-of-pearl and covered in scraps of
African kuba cloth. All of the chairs and one side table are
on casters so that guests can move them to create dining
or entertaining clusters; the stationary larger pieces frame
the space. The design goal of "a room for reading, visiting
with friends, and dining" is attained with this flexibility.

(opposite) **Focusing in on a corner of the living room reveals how harmony can
be achieved by mixing and contrasting fabrics. Lots of subtle textures in
juxtaposition can work together to express harmony.**

(following pages) **An eclectic array of furnishings, fabrics, and styles work to create a casual, comfortable, and colorful living room and dining area. The room
accommodates the preferences of guests and spur-of-the-moment chat circles
because the accent chairs and an occasional table are on casters.**

(above) **A shallow table skirted in linen dresses up the passageway to a home office, showcases an art collection, and yields conveniently-hidden extra storage space.**

(opposite) **A pair of white wood side tables created by the designer frame a bed. Notice how the pulls are painted to look like leather luggage handles.**

Photos: Pieter Estersohn

light and fluid space

Jennifer Post

When the owner of this 3,800-square-foot (342-square-meter) Manhattan condominium took Jennifer Post for a pre-rehab tour, the design flaws were obvious: it was dark and it had no character. However, the original space was a gem, located in a landmark building overlooking a lake in Central Park. Post concluded it needed three ingredients to come into its own: light, height, and fluidity—elements, from an architectural and design standpoint, needed to create clean lines. Post calls this the "Armani attitude." Clean means no-frills, unadorned architecture in which to achieve simple, modern, minimalist space.

Walls were knocked down and the ceiling and doorway heights raised to bring in light, views, and to create the fluidity Post strives for. The living room and dining room became a single huge room with 180-degree views of Central Park. The result is a house that opens outward, "a castle in the sky." The finishes prevent the eye from fixing on any one detail or line. The windows have no drapes, just sheers to keep out ultraviolet rays. Cabinets are linear and the baseboards have no reveals; all the hardware is stainless steel and all the fabrics monochromatic. Such freedom and fluidity, so rare in an urban environment, kindle warmth and comfort.

(right) **All of the walls are painted with Post's signature high gloss white except for the faux lizard pattern which blankets this foyer wall. A semi-honed marble floor complements this small oasis of color.**

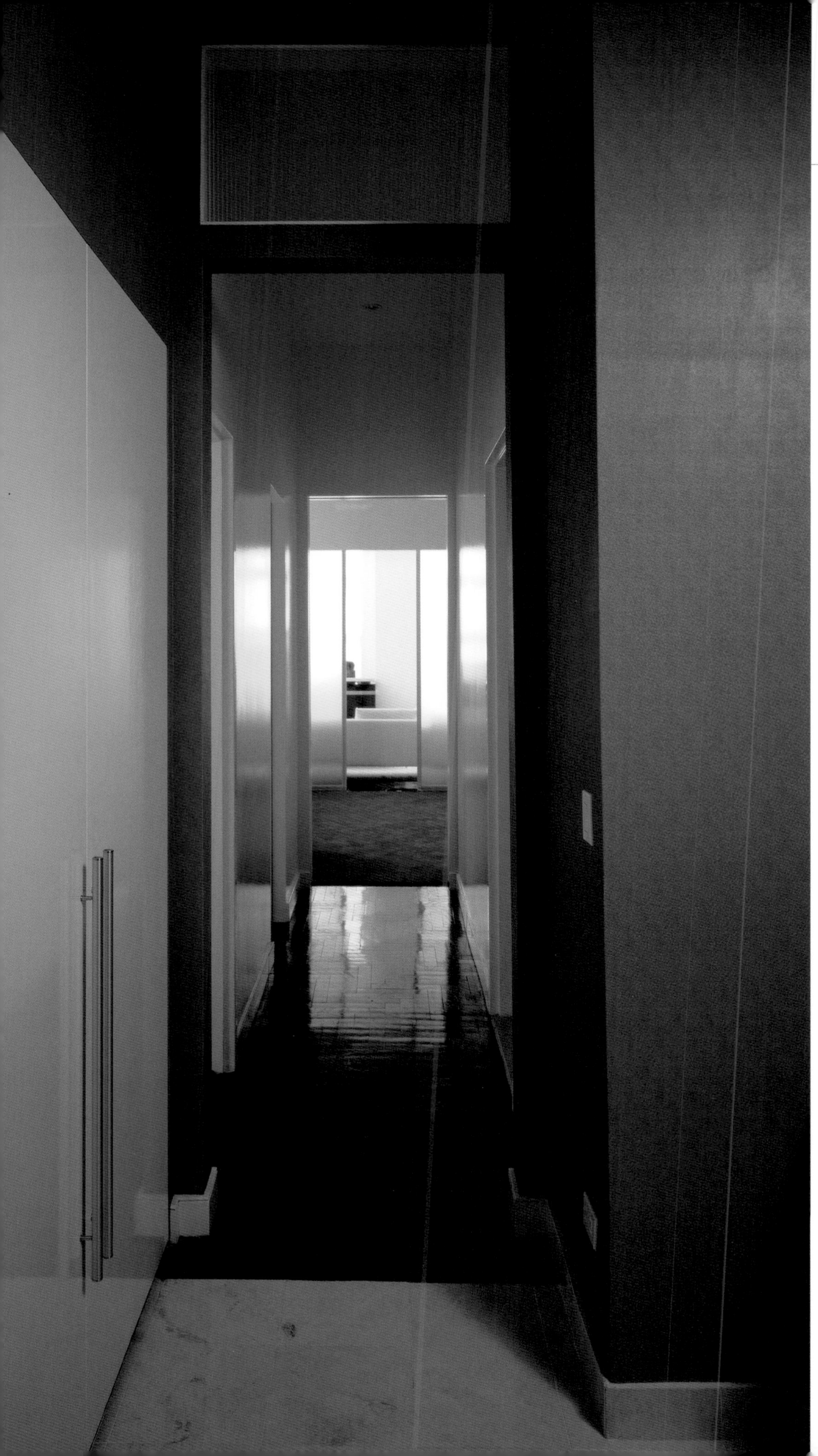

In this city hideaway, walls are painted a high-gloss white
so that natural light bounces every which way, perpetuat-
ing the visual movement created by the minimal finishes.
The faux lizard finish, which blankets the foyer walls, is the
exception; it was selected here to make the space look
larger. The marble floor complements this micro-oasis of
color, but it is set back in a semi-honed finish to mute any
Las Vegas-like glitz. The darkest color in the palette, the
high-gloss cocoa stain on the floors, introduces an element
of classic design, a touch of prewar style, and contrasts
with the modern minimalism elsewhere. The fabrics are
natural textured cottons and wools. The hand-loomed
cotton Indian rugs play with light and contrast with the
cocoa floor to register yet another level of visual interest in
this fascinating space.

(above) **The living room, which overlooks the blue of a Central Park lake,
expresses a minimalist mood. Pristine white furniture sits quietly in the background, floating like small, suspended glaciers over a high-gloss cocoa floor.**

(right) **Simplicity and drama are combined in this sleek cabinet crowned with
a magnificent, clean-lined mirror that reflects activity as much as it does
natural light. Tiny lights on a micro-thin rail move about the room with the sub-
tlety of flickering stars.**

(right) **The living room's view of the Manhattan skyline at night adds a touch of romance to the candlelit room.**

a summer cottage is reborn

When the old summer cottage of a Massachusetts family had to come down, they decided to rebuild on the same plot of oceanfront land. Their goal was to borrow design elements from

Albert, Righter & Tittman Architects, Inc.

both the cottage and the family's year-round farmhouse residence, while creating a new cottage which would look at home among the old Greek Revival houses in the neighborhood. The assignment went to Boston architect Jacob D. Albert.

The new cottage's rooms were designed not to focus on outside views, but rather to correspond with their use. On summer evenings and during the winter, the family congregates indoors for meals and relaxing. To accommodate this, Albert created rooms that are cozy, comfortable retreats. In keeping with the owners' preference for merging the old with the new and maintaining a spare aesthetic, the rooms are simple, allowing just a few meaningful architectural details to shine through—like V-groove wood paneling and a natural-finish pine floor throughout the house.

The main floor comprises a kitchen, half bath, dining room, living room, library, mud room, laundry, storage area, and screened porch. The space is casual, so no formal entry or front door was built; people come in through the mud room, or the porch, if they're coming in from the beach. The second floor has four bedrooms and two baths. Downstairs, the continuity of the dining room and kitchen keeps the mood informal and facilitates serving large groups. The hand-painted backsplash behind the kitchen sink complements the dining room rug and suggests that the two rooms function as one. High ceilings with recessed lighting and a restrained use of furnishings keep the look of the dining room big, spacious, and clean.

The owner wanted to keep the space as maintenance-free as possible. The kitchen walls are plastered and the backsplash is hand-painted with stripes to mimic old beadboard.

(right) **Typical of the design theme in this Cape Cod getaway, a mix of styles merges on a visual plane. A Warren Platner chair is adjacent to an antique drop-leaf table; the details of both shine through in this simple setting of wood and white.**

(following page, left) **The gray top of the fire-slate work island breaks up the white of the cabinetry in the kitchen. Used in chemistry labs, fire-slate is tough, yet also easy to clean and maintain; it is a perfect choice for a busy beach house with lots of cooks.**

(following page, right) **Family heirloom chairs are set tight against the dining room table, which is made from old boards; seating is augmented by two new leather chairs. The striped Woodard cotton rug sets off the seating area, adds color to the room, and complements the striped chair covers.**

Photos: Sam Ogden

Most of the countertops are a simple laminate, but the work island is made from fire slate, which is traditionally used in chemistry labs. It cannot be cut or scratched, and when stained, it takes on a character that the owners like. Much of the lighting is hidden in the ceiling, out of the way, and the stairs are subtly illuminated by tiny bulbs located under the handrail. In keeping with the clean theme, all walls are China white.

The owners preferred to furnish the cottage by integrating meaningful old pieces with new ones. For example, a Warren Platner chair sits at the base of the staircase next to an antique drop-leaf table topped with a new Zen light. The dining room table, made from old boards, is anchored by two new leather chairs and sits atop a Woodard cotton rag rug. The couch, side chairs, and wicker furniture in the library are all family pieces that came from either the farm or the original cottage.

(right) **When the family brought the old furniture into the beach house library, the wicker was white—but with 9-foot(3-meter)-plus ceilings and white walls, the effect was too cold. To warm the room, the wicker was painted green and the cushions and couch were covered in similarly earthy tones.**

Photos: Sam Ogden

Architect Michael Gabellini has a passion for archeology and has spent much time studying the daily and domestic life of ancient civilizations. Gabellini is particularly interested in the construction of urban space and the connection between public and private spaces via courtyards and palazzos. "So much of what I see abroad exemplifies pleasure in space, and it seems much more rational, logical, flexible, and self-supporting with the home as a sanctuary," he says. In his travels, the plans and details of historic buildings often resurface in his architecture.

Gabellini Associates

One such project is the transformation of a 3500-square-foot (315-square-meter) Park Avenue penthouse with four exposures and three 1000-square-foot (90-square-meter) terraces overlooking Manhattan. Citing his historical inspiration, Gabellini recalled a fifteenth-century monastery he had seen in Europe that had changed over the course of 800 years into a prison, a law court, and back to a monastery. Gabellini sought to recreate the flexibility of its simple floor plan, centered around an interior courtyard, in this Manhattan space.

The design intent was to make this home a "celebration of pleasure" where the owners' exquisite collection of twentieth-century photography could occupy center stage. To accomplish this, the material palette reflects the tones of a vintage platinum print, providing a muted, complementary backdrop.

A serene field of space is defined by a white plaster ceiling and the continuous Arria limestone floor three- by three-foot (1- by 1-meter) panels. The spaces within are defined by the perimeter plaster walls and what Gabellini calls "courtyard walls" of ebony ribbon mahogany that set off the living room, study, and master bedroom.

The courtyards are lit by the glow from three glass-enclosed bathrooms. Full-height translucent glass walls separate each bathroom from adjacent spaces; in the master bath, the walls and sliding door are made from low-voltage, privacy glass that transforms from clear to opaque with the touch of a switch.

Throughout the apartment, museum-quality lighting illuminates not only the artwork but the space itself. In addition, the system includes elements of theatrical

(opposite) **The courtyard dining room is set against a pier of ribbon mahogany; a satin stainless steel server cantilevers off the pier. The table, honed-finished bluestone, on a stainless steel pedestal, stands quietly against the Arria limestone floor. The walnut and natural-fiber dining chairs by George Nakashima offer warmth to the surrounding cool tones.**

lighting which can alter the mood of the space. For example, if it is raining, the lights inside can be adjusted to erase the gloom and create a glow. It is even possible to suggest moonlight when that mood is called for. In essence, the space is designed to present "an individual portrait of the owners' life." It is space edited by them and for them. While the work could be described as minimalist, Gabellini prefers opulent "in terms of indulging the senses."

(right and above) **The architect created the master bath after hearing about baths the owners had seen and taken note of during their travels around the world. With the touch of a switch, this glass box master bath can transform from translucent to clear, depending on the mood of the owners. It is a place to pamper the body.**

(following pages) **The living room is furnished with modern classics such as the Saporiti sofa. The chairs, by designer Yoshio Tamiguchi, are reproductions from Tokyo's Hotel Okura created at the owner's request. The stainless steel table is a Gabellini design.**

Photo: Paul Warchol

Architect Scott Bromley's year-round weekend home, not too far from his Manhattan offices, is on nearby Fire Island. The unusual octagonal waterside getaway is the antithesis

R. Scott Bromley

of his city loft, which is in an old converted button factory.

The island home, a 1962 creation of designer Gifford Drew, consists of two distinct structures: a main house, set off by 10- by 10-foot (3- by 3-meter) pavilions, and a teahouse in the middle of the garden. It is the perfect spot for reading and gazing out over the bay, or for entertaining. It can easily accommodate eight for dining. The whole setup is reminiscent of Bali.

A distinctive character of the home is its simplicity and the open, airy feeling that comes with one deck after another wrapping all eight sides of the structure. The views of the water and the gardens, which feature natural grasses, mature plants, and grapevines, add to the peaceful mood. The only structural changes made to the space over the years were the addition of a dining room—once the back deck—and a guest suite, separated from the dining area by basketweave poplar wood panels, courtesy of Bromley's design team. The inside shingles were stained to match the outside, and the floor was tinted a hue that picks up the lighter tones in the shingles.

The very Bali living room, which looks like a massive, monotone tent is a favorite of Bromley's. In the summer, the peaked ceiling catches the hot air swirling up from all the doors on the main floor and keeps the room cool. The only rooms with real windows are the kitchen and the bath; the rest of the light and air comes in via the doors.

There is not much furniture or infusions of color in this home, and with that comes a distinct calm. The white couch in the living room is really two beds that Bromley merged and then upholstered in Sunbrella fabric. A simple milk crate painted black serves as a micro-coffee table. In the dining room, the old rough cedar table that came with the house was retained because of its perfect fit; it is kept waxed to a high sheen.

The Bertoia chairs in the dining room introduce a black accent and are so comfortable that guests linger at the table for hours on end. In keeping with the relaxed beach mood, a low-maintenance, fossil floor lines the house. The kitchen, which faces east, receives wonderful light on sunny summer days. The simple, butcher-block countertops and the trio of banker's lights are original to the home and continue to function well. This is a great place to prepare a meal; the views are addictive, and the smell of the sea air is intoxicating.

(opposite) **This open, airy Bali-esque room is one of Bromley's favorites. In the summer, the hot air rises to the peak and cool air easily circulates below as a result of the many openings in the octagon. In winter, the Scandinavian wood stove in the corner keeps guests warm.**

(previous pages, left) **An old cedar wood table that came with the house continues to work as a dining room table, and the simple black chairs from Bertoia
are so comfortable that guests can chat here until the sun comes up. In keeping with the open floor layout, the guest bedroom is separated by only a
simple basketweave screen, which Bromley's firm designed and built.**

(previous pages, right) **The teahouse, a few steps from the main house, sits in
the middle of a thick, green garden—a little hideaway with magical views. The
furniture is made from two-by-four wood planks and the small end tables can
instantly stack and hold a tabletop for a dinner for eight.**

(right) **The kitchen, one of the 10- by 10-foot (3- by 3-meter) pavilions off the center room of this octagonal complex, is filled with natural light and surrounded
by the greenery outside. Its beauty comes from its simplicity and its function-
ality when preparing and cooking a summer meal.**

Photos: John Hall

a handmade home for useable art

Linda Chase

Designer Linda Chase's front-door key is about 5 inches (12 cm) long and unlocks her prized little Haddam, Connecticut, Federal home that dates to 1817. The quirky key—the size of a small hand—symbolizes Chase's love of craftsmanship and the spirit of people who make things by hand. The wholesome environment—five acres of bucolic scenes, complete with sheep and cows—is an appropriate setting for this handmade home and the objects within it.

The house expresses the designer's style: lyrical fabrics, infusions of "lipstick and fashion colors," unexpected design elements, and rooms that hold a person's history and distinct personality in full view. The grand proportions and simplicity of the rooms—the building was originally a parsonage—provide the perfect backdrop for unusual furniture pieces, collections of porcelain and books, and striking color accents of burnt orange and piercing purples. Architectural proportion and unexpected color are a perfect design duo—as seen in the little bands of pink and yellow trailing around the walls.

"Unless I am in a museum, I don't get excited over rooms that are reproductions, and I am bothered by rooms that are too precious and appointed," Chase says. The goal was to fill the home with objects, collected over the years, in a way that would be interesting, fun to live with, touchable,

(left) **An eclectic collection of antique pieces, including a wonderful old painted armoire, circle this one-of-a-kind bed. A collection of antique books—one pile topped with a pair of antique dress shoes—and a mantelpiece collection of early photographs add detail and texture.**

and even practical. Some design rules do pertain: scale, proportion, balance, and symmetry. These were followed in the placement of furniture, objects, and other design elements throughout the home.

Chase readily admits to a "chair fetish" because, like no other piece of furniture, chairs project human qualities and distinct personalities through the arms and legs. "I'm a very down-to-earth person, and there's a warmth, honesty, and freedom about these pieces. I feel you cannot make a mistake decorating with the things you love. If it's honest, it's good," she says.

(above) **This former parsonage's mood had been very somber, but the simplicity of its clean walls, free of detail, made a blank canvas for dashes of color and whimsical wall panels.**

(right) **Electric purple chairs glow in the dining room, beckoning guests. Hand-painted panels decorate the walls. The limited and simple furnishings focus well-deserved attention on the original mantel and on the porcelain collection arrayed on an antique buffet.**

(following pages) **When seeking to create additional workspace in her kitchen, rather than constructing an island counter—an expected solution—Chase chose an antique French apothecary cabinet with lots of handy drawers for storage. Wicker baskets, placed underneath, make an easy-to-reach toy box. The piece conveys an irresistible spirit.**

Photos: David Phelps

When we think of Maine architecture, the traditional clapboard farmhouse comes to mind. But this Maine home has none of those familiar design elements, inside or out. It is

Winton Scott Architects

a sprawling, modern seaside residence in the middle of a meadow—in all, a twenty-acre (eight-hectare) parcel that sweeps down to a sandy beach. When Winton Scott describes the ultra-customized rooms, views, balconies, courtyard, subterranean glass-roofed pool, and indoor overhead bridges, the home begins to sound dreamlike. But this unique creation is used year-round by a family, and all the customizing serves them well. To arrive at the final design, Scott conducted a detailed analysis of the family's needs and desires. For example, the owners wanted to be able to take their morning coffee on a balcony off the master bedroom, so Scott designed a 3-foot(1-meter)-square balcony to accommodate this requirement. In winter, they can move to their sitting room; for a more westerly view, another balcony is nearby. The many terraces and balconies are points at which people can move from the inside out, each with a different view. It is obvious that the owners cherish the natural landscape as much as the rooms within the home.

A broader requirement was for a Maine version of the sun-catching courtyards and shady arcades the family had admired in Latin America. The courtyard thus is built with its back to the cold winter winds and features an outdoor fireplace that provides a protected outdoor space, even in the dead of winter. Another year-round escape is the indoor pool, which is partially covered by earth and warmed by sunlight though a glass roof.

The core of the house is open and airy with curving walls and stairways that contrast with the hard edges. The interior design goal was to create autonomously functioning rooms that are visually connected from the ground floor up. As a result, one can see many rooms at once. Views to the courtyard and beyond help maintain the connection to the outdoors. The clay tile flooring is imported from Mexico; as the house uses a radiant heating system, the tiles are literally the heating elements. A dark clay was chosen for its ability to hold heat.

A massive fireplace holds the focus in the living room; the stone is hand-selected and native to northern New England, and is used for the outside retaining walls as well. The car-sized stones at the base of the fireplace gradually give way to smaller stones as it climbs the high wall. The wood throughout is Douglas fir, except for the narrow detail strips on the walls and bookshelf, which are African mahogany.

(opposite) **A curving, wood staircase leads to the upstairs bedrooms. Open views appear through six big windows that climb alongside. Skylights, clay tile, wrought-iron artwork in a marine motif—all surrounded by magnificent woodwork—tempt one to stop and toast to craftsmanship.**

At the top of the curving staircase to the second floor, a bridge separates the master bedroom wing from the children's. Soaking tubs, whirlpool baths, skylit showers, and numerous built-ins in the bedrooms make these rooms getaways within a getaway. The playful wrought-iron railing, which depicts all kinds of marine life, was created by a local artist. The little stairway behind the fireplace leads to a home office complete with a customized mahogany desk.

(below) **Situated in an open meadow with unobstructed views of the ocean, this modern mansion on twenty acres (eight hectares) holds many an architectural surprise inside. Every room unfolds into another, each with its own view and unique qualities.**

(opposite) **Car-sized rocks formed the base of this massive stone fireplace. The fire and the radiant heat caught in the clay floor tiles keep this room warm during the coldest Maine winters.**

(following pages) **Another smoothly curving architectural detail, this time a bookcase, creates a sweeping wave of mahogany and fir in this passageway.**

Photos: James R. Salomon

Here was the ultimate project for an interior designer: give a fresh look to a potato barn turned cow barn turned home. A working farm for twenty-five years, the two-acre lot in

Zina Glazebrook

East Hampton, New York (complete with three integrated silos) was once part of a working dairy on a 120-acre (48-hectare) parcel. The bright red, two-story home is nestled deep in the green of a mature lawn and partially wrapped in privet evergreens. To the south, the view is enhanced by a typical white country fence and open views to the sea. Roses and daylilies provide splashes of color along the way.

When Zina Glazebrook took on the assignment, the thought was to appraise the home's features and do a simple design clean-up. Having grown up in a livestock barn turned home herself, the designer was excited at the creative possibilities. Before she was through, she worked on many rooms in this unique living space.

The first room needing a major change was the kitchen, which was "too complex" and full of terra-cotta tiles. The nickname "House by Tequila" was short-lived! Glazebrook and the owner often brainstormed via magazine tearsheets depicting ideas the owner liked. Out of that exercise came a concept the designer calls "primitive modernism" that embraces the materials that were used in the barn and similar rustic structures.

For example, the front door to the main entry silo is made of harvested driftwood from an old dock that washed up on the shores of Montauk, New York. An old grain store door works as the privacy door in the master bath. Rather than being torn up, the old hayloft floor on the second floor was refurbished with an oil-based urethane to a beautiful affect.

To keep the barn mood, the kitchen floor was power-troweled like terrazzo; heat radiates via hot water and rubber hoses installed below the surface. The custom kitchen cabinets resemble utility cabinets one would see in a barn; nickel and limestone accents are integrated in the room. Prior to choosing a stove, Glazebrook consulted with a chef who highly recommended a hefty restaurant stove called the Grizzly, by Montague; it cost less than $3,000 and has six burners, a griddle, grill, and two major ovens. The look is perfect in this utilitarian kitchen.

Oversized butler's sinks from England were chosen for the kitchen and are perfect for cleaning up after a crowd! The idea came from a friend who once used a bathtub as a sink. The wooden chairs around the kitchen table are from Indonesia; they were found at a warehouse sale. The sixty-inch (152-cm) round table is made from a Palladian

(opposite) **Here is half of the Palladian window from the living room, this time serving as a tabletop. It is covered in sandblasted glass for easy care and cleanup. The simple wooden chairs that surround it are Indonesian; they were found at a warehouse sale.**

courthouse window; half of it was set on a poured-concrete column and topped with a half inch of sand-blasted glass for a table, and the other half became a window in the living room.

The bathroom fixtures were found in London and are old kitchen sinks with drainboards that give guests a spacious ledge for toiletries. The master bath features a six-foot (2-meter) turn-of-the-century tub; the shower has a big, modern head with an output that feels like a rainstorm over the body.

Most furnishings for the house were purchased at yard sales, flea markets, or warehouse sales. The exception is the guest beds that Glazebrook designed and built with burlap and raffia upholstery; they are twin beds that can easily be merged into a king-sized bed. The walls are painted with Benjamin Moore Super White throughout, and all window treatments are the same simple, inexpensive Swiss cotton roller shades.

(above) **A six-foot (2-meter) turn-of-the-century tub from London fills the window span in the master bath.**

(opposite) **An old Palladian window salvaged from a courthouse brings the country view inside. It looks like the center of a sparkling gem. The low, identical Donghia sofas accented with deep purple pillows draw the eye to this light-filled sitting area.**

Photos: Michael Mundy

At first glance, this home, which sits in the middle of a big meadow with open sea views, looks like every other old Maine farm—but this is not a farm and the construction is new. The buildings include a main house, a garage that resembles a barn, and an art studio that looks like it could house farm equipment. For architect Matt Elliott, the idea of transforming this huge field into personal space, bringing it to an intimate scale, felt right.

Elliott & Elliott Architecture

The interior design goal was to keep the space as clean as the Maine air and as open as the views. "We treated the inside almost like a renovation, like an old shell that was getting a contemporary look. All the rooms look into each other and are very subtly defined," Elliott says. The tall windows, nine feet (three meters) high, are proportionately correct for the sizes of the rooms and saturate all the space in light and views. Finishes are simple, clean, and Shaker-like. The walls are painted a matte white, bringing out design elements like the rich tones of the granite on the fireplace. When possible, local products were used; the fireplace granite, for example, is from Deer Isle.

But perhaps the most distinctive design characteristic is the way everything is treated as a movable object—a concept that meant "no built-ins" to the owners. The granite fireplace purposefully sits six inches (15 cm) from the wall; as do the sink and mirror in the master bath and the cast-iron heating units, all like freestanding sculptures. Even the island of cabinetry in the dining room sits away from the wall. According to Elliott, he and his associates spent a great deal of time looking for the right hardware for the cabinets, but finally decided that the best design would be to have none so they simply drilled holes in the doors, then sanded and painted them. A warm, brown granite caps the cabinets and maintains the clean look. Even the fireplace flue is treated as an art object, a big, clean, reflective silver tube that moves from the living room up into the master bedroom.

Most lighting is handled by lamps, except for an exposed cathode tube that runs the entire length of the first floor. Furnishings all came from the owners' past. The wooden coffee table in the living room, for example, was once used to store fireplace logs and was a hand-me-down. The couch

(opposite) **Huge, bare windows that frame the meadow and ocean views resemble hung art in a magical gallery that changes with the time of day or season. The clean, uncluttered views inside bring attention to the simple furnishings, mostly garage and barn sale finds. The exception is the little stool to the right of the flue, which is a hand-me-down from the owner's grandmother.**

and chairs from the 1920s and 1930s were purchased at garage sales. A big-print fabric on the couch, however, was replaced by a good shade of white. An unusual white and brown bureau in the master bedroom is the owners' answer to contemporary style housed in an antique form.

Above all, the design of this home succeeds in the main goal of preserving the views. The magnificent vistas are never obstructed; there are no window treatments. "You could make a career out of looking out the windows," the owner says.

(above) **This view demonstrates the open architecture and the imaginative way a simple storage area can define and separate one room from another. To the right, an open metal staircase leads to the second-floor master bedroom and bath. The handrail and treads are maple to match the floors. Clear panels keep the views intact while guarding the stairs that lead to the downstairs storage area.**

(opposite) **The unusual one-piece sink and mirror frame their own space and create a functional sculpture. The cool silver complements the gray granite in the shower stall and other fixtures. One solid piece of granite covers the floor and another the walls. The pale green modesty panel, a reminder of sea glass found at the ocean's edge, shuts off the shower room. His and hers toilets flank the 6- by 6-foot (2- by 2-meter) shower room.**

(following pages) **The living room maintains the neutral palette, leaving the dominating color scheme to nature's whim, and holds the simplicity intact with a minimal amount of furnishings. It is hard to imagine feeling anything but at peace here. Notice how the maple floors hold the glow of the sun and define the interior space.**

Photos: Brian Vanden Brink

Interior designer Laura Bohn loved the idea that this second-floor loft space was unfinished, without partitions dividing the huge space. She took 2,200 square feet

Laura Bohn

(180 square meters)—not in a straight line—of the floor and proceeded to design a home for her husband, herself, and their two dogs. Her selection included ten windows, four by eight feet (1.2 by 2.4 meters) each, which wrap the front corner of the space and drench it with sunlight. Together with the high ceilings, they led the designer to keep the plan open, without traditional walls. Instead, partitions delineate rooms; even the master bedroom floats freely in the space, set behind a curved partition.

To add interest and accommodate plumbing, an entry hall was added, the ceiling lowered, and the floor was raised—now one enters the main space stepping down. The flooring is a pre-finished, high-gloss maple typically used on gymnasium floors. It is set on rubber padding for a little bounce that makes it pleasant to walk on.

The dining area, which doubles as a breakfast nook, is also on a raised portion of the space. It is floored with an inexpensive ceramic tile and edged in a solid piece of limestone. Bohn designed the table, which is made from rough-cut cedar that was soaked for three days, rubbed with a wash, and then sealed. The result is a "rustic refined" material perched on a non-wood base. A hand-painted gold canvas chair from Donghia gives some

warmth to the corner, and the John Boone couch was purchased because it was a perfect fit for the space.

The green and blue palette is evident in everything from the pillows to the painting. It works its way right into the living room, where comfortable overstuffed chairs and couches sit in a circle of sunlight and dashes of green and blue guide the eye around the room. There is nothing fancy, nothing extra, and no furnishings steal the show. The room seems to be all about comfort, calm, and an understated, simple look. The quiet beige fabrics covering the couches vary from painter's canvas to linen.

The ceramic tile carries through from the dining area to the kitchen. The metal mica cabinetry is a soft aluminum and includes screen doors and open shelves for easy access to frequently used items. The cabinets over the refrigerator and sink are flat faced to keep the visual plane clean. The cooking island was treated like a piece of furniture—hence the curves—and is capped in honed granite. The counters are covered in honed Carrara marble. Walls here are done in Ralph Lauren taupe gray suede paint; all other walls have a shiny finish to reflect light throughout the space.

All kinds of light fixtures and bulbs are mixed and matched throughout the house. They range from halogen to incandescent bulbs, with lamps and fixtures that produce either yellow or white light, and providing a choice depending on the mood desired.

The master bath is a wonderful creation that picks up on the open theme by placing the shower stall in the middle of the room. The cozy wrap of milky white subway tiles mixed in with diamond and square shapes is covered in Venetian plaster, which resembles marble. The walls are powder blue and, along with the mirrored walls, give the room depth and keep it looking cool.

(previous pages and above) **The light wood floors, the same pre-finished maple used in gymnasiums, glistens in the sun with its high sheen; it sits on rubber pads, which makes for a nice bounce. The floor sets off the circle of furniture, which looks like sculptures in sand. Big squares of pale color tossed in via pillows look rooted, like surreal plantings. The expanses of pale blue and green walls lift the room to the light.**

(opposite) **The end of a corridor is capped with a pleasant collage of textures, color, and art.**

(right) **As there are no closed walls in the main space, it made perfect design sense to carry the theme through to the bath. Tiny subway tiles are set in patterns within the shower stall, creating the illusion of a knitted wall of stone. The designer created the curve with Venetian plaster, which reads as marble. The bright blue stool to the left breaks up the walls of white and is covered in an iridescent polyester fabric from Jack Larson. A rubbed metal mica cabinet sits back in the design scheme, edged against a polished Carrara marble vanity.**

Photos: Michael Dunne

When designer Mary Douglas Drysdale began working with these clients, art was the focus of their home. The problem was, it seemed their entire vast collection was on display

Mary Douglas Drysdale

so pieces competed with one another and none got the attention they deserved. When the couple moved to new, spacious quarters in Washington, D.C., Drysdale was chosen to design a home to accommodate and show their art collection. She made the walls a neutral, warm white so all the pieces would stand out. Drysdale also designed a nearly

invisible storage system that allows easy access to the art, which is displayed on a rotating basis. In addition, a wall grid supports an orderly art viewing system. Part of the design plan backfired though because the owners fell in love with the clean wall grids and opted to keep them bare! Instead, pedestals in the form of furniture, a mantel, and a room divider became natural showcases for the contemporary glass collection.

A three-story atrium topped by a magnificent, huge skylight pours light over the space. On the first level, the mirrored cubbyhole separating the two doors shows off more art in reality, and in reflection. This room is literally an in-home gallery that can be transformed into entertaining space or an auxiliary dining room. In the quest for order and balance, the elevator door to the right of the mirror is repeated on the left in painted trompe l'oeil. The light wood table with nickel inlay was created by the designer as a gift for her clients. The table centers the atrium and serves as a casual display venue for small art pieces.

On the second level, in the living room, blond wood furniture sits back and colorful glass art punctuates corners and tabletops. The coffee table, the console by the window, and the fireplace are all Drysdale creations. The

owners requested that their cat's desire to sunbathe be considered, so a little ledge was incorporated under the console. A soft, waterfall Roman shade in silk filters the light and facilitates a seamless transition between the room's architecture and its interior decoration.

The kitchen is a functional galley-style room that trails to a light-filled tip, a natural spot for dining. For color and smiles, painter Rebecca Cross introduced a chili pepper theme, reflecting a favorite cooking ingredient of the owners. New Orleans artist and furniture maker Mario Villa created the kitchen chairs with vine-like twists of wrought iron with a touch of gold. The colorful tablecloth is a Drysdale creation of hand sewn color squares. "I've always focused on things custom and handmade, and on creating my own patterns and forms. This way clients have something unique to their home," she says.

(previous pages, left) **A passion of this designer is detail, right down to the fabric. This custom-designed and -appliquéd pillow was created from the designer's own drawing, based on Renaissance metalwork.**

(previous pages, right) **Light pours down the skylight into three stories, of which two function as a gallery and entertainment area. With neutral walls and lots of open space, each piece of art can be viewed without distraction.**

(right) **Part of the designer's goal was to create an orderly art viewing system, which resulted in the wall grids seen here. However, the owners liked the clean, spare look so much they left the grids plain and clean, focusing instead on tabletop art. Notice the cat snuggled against the window to the left; this sunbathing ledge was designed by special request.**

Photos: Andrew Lautman

Interior designer Rick Berns found this contemporary, cedar saltbox beach house on Fire Island irresistible. A

Berns Fry Interiors

simple structure, it was nestled in the woods with a screened in porch that made it look as though it were frozen in time.

In planning the interior design, Bern's goal, he says, was to give the house a "beachy, always-been-there" look. He wanted to hold the same mood and feel that the porch captured. Some deconstruction was necessary to simplify and cleanup the design. For example, he decided to remove some faux Victorian fans from the ceiling. And because he already had the benefit of a pleasant, private outdoor space, he decided to enhance the views with the help of landscape designer Ricks Lee. Lee's work capitalized on the existing verdure, resulting in a seamless whole between home and environment.

The wonderful old porch needed no alteration, just some interesting furniture and old pieces to make it a more useful living space. The legs of the antique table are made from logs that came out of an old barn. The chairs, a mix of painted, Victorian bamboo and pre-Civil War pieces, including the armchair, were found in a funky junk store in North Carolina. They are all painted the same color, but each is a slightly different height.

The theme in the living room is casual and eclectic. Seating includes an old leather-covered butterfly chair and two cushy, single-reed, bamboo-armed chairs covered in white sailcloth. The couches are covered in canvas cloth and the simple, clean white seating area is defined by a big, bold cowhide rug. Furnishings, both on the porch and inside, comprise a collection of Bern's favorite finds from auctions and flea markets.

Notice the narrow sawhorse table that displays the artwork. Berns thinks it had some industrial application in its past. To make the inside views compelling, he aligns works by well-known photographers with flea-market specials. The only theme here is that all the photos are in black and white. A collage of other art pieces is nearby, and two towering, nineteenth-century black iron urns dominate the scheme. The tobacco barn ladder, a precious find, adds color and texture to the white wall of the living room. On a sunny day, the shadows that climb the wall add an interesting dimension.

Regardless of what he collects or adds to his home, Berns says, "nothing is so precious that it can't come and go." He

(opposite) **This weathered looking porch seems light years from Manhattan, and that is just what drew designer Rick Berns to this house. He kept the country feeling by choosing furnishings that look like they have been here for years.**

enjoys the freedom to introduce his new discoveries, and sometimes replace or rotate old ones. In keeping with his desire to always freshen the look, photographs and art are not hung. That way he can change the look instantly. He says the neutral palette and the no-clutter rule keeps the focus in his home on the energy that people and activity bring to a room—just where he believes the emphasis should be.

(above) **Berns likes to have the option to change his interior views, so he keeps his art off the walls for easy rotation. The only art theme is that all the photography is black and white.**

(opposite) **There is no place to climb in this room. The tobacco barn ladder, an antique store find, is here to add texture and interesting shadows.**

(following pages) **The designer pulled together an eclectic and comfortable look for the living room. It is interesting to look at, but for him, it is not as important as the people who come to visit, bringing life and energy.**

Photos: Pieter Estersohn

Interior designer Lee Bogart had the advantage every designer covets—to know the clients very well. This precludes the need for spending time on the getting-to-know-you stage, which can lengthen the creative process significantly. In fact, Bogart had already worked with this family on designing their New York apartment and their first home. She knew the wife of the couple quite well in terms of design likes and dislikes, and knew all of her palette passions.

Lee Bogart

Bogart's goal for this sprawling seaside retreat on Long Island was to aid in the execution of her clients' many design ideas so that the home's interior did not look obviously decorated. The new structure was designed and built by the architectural firm Kean Williams Giambertone of Cold Springs Harbor, New York. The turn-of-the-century, shingled cottage boasts water views from nearly every window and lots of porch space. That, combined with the family's passion for all things nautical, inspired both architect and designer.

In the two-level family room, for example, there is a seating area Bogart calls the "crow's nest," which is reached by a spiral staircase; one can perch and watch the activity on the Sound during the day and gaze at the stars all night. A simple seating arrangement of two leather chairs facing the water dominates the light-filled loft. From below, in the lower level of the family room, the impression is that one is in the hull of a massive boat being readied for a virgin sail.

Furnishings are simple and casual and include a Thorndike sofa in distressed leather from the Ralph Lauren Home Collection. Two comfortable, overstuffed chairs face the water. The red, flat wool rug in tweed and the plaid pillows carry the owners' palette choices of raspberry, yellow, blue, green, and red in various degrees. According to Bogart, the man of the house wanted every seat in this room to be especially comfortable.

The kitchen is open to the family room and takes advantage of the views as well as the spectacular light. Hardwood floors contrast with the simple white cabinetry, accented with brass pulls and hardware. Countertops are of dark green granite that compliments the small checkerboard tile trail. Other areas feature raised tiles decorated with fish and crabs. All tiles are from Country Floors.

A private study was completed in earthy greens, from the couches to the star-patterned rug from Stark. Here, the husband retires with friends to enjoy a cigar or sherry. The couches, covered in green sailcloth, came from the family's first house, as did the little table, an antique ammunition box. Notice the model of the U.S.S. Constitution and the pillow with the fish print adding to the nautical mood.

(opposite) **With views like this, it is hard to imagine the family is ever inside when summer arrives. Even the terrier enjoys the sea air and breezes.**

(above) **Here is a unique room divider. This five-foot(1.5 meter)-long glass enclosure houses a model of the 1930 America's Cup Yankee yacht from the Mystic Connecticut Maritime Gallery.**

(opposite) **The family room and what the designer calls the "crow's nest," a lookout area at the top of the spiral staircase, feature a nautical theme in what could be a luxury boat's hull.**

(following pages) **With the kitchen open to the family room, traffic and conversation move freely room to room. Simple wood cabinets with brass closures, topped in green granite, keep the workspace clean and uncluttered.**

Photos: Pieter Estersohn, courtesy of *House & Garden*, Condé Naste Publications, Inc.

a new look for a new life

Benjamin Noriega-Ortiz

Sometimes, when people's lives change, they feel the need to change their homes as well and they look to interior designers to help freshen and make the space work better. In the case of this Manhattan apartment, the children had grown up and left home, and the owners' life focus had changed. Their home became less a place for nurture than a space where entertaining, social events, and meetings were held. They called on renowned designer Benjamin Noriega-Ortiz for help in shedding the Park Avenue traditional look of chintz, opaque drapes, and dark, woody antiques. They wanted the house to be comfortable and more open to the new visitors they expected.

One of the first steps was to remove some of the antiques and all of the heavy opaque drapes that darkened the space. Taking a cue from the owners' interest in lampshades, the designer created a very special one for the entryway, gluing ostrich feathers to fabric and dyeing them to match the palette. The lamp was then set on a big round table covered in metallic mitered silk, set in turn on a custom-made rug with a feather pattern. The mitered fabric, where the stripes go in different directions, makes the table shimmer in the light and seem as though it could

(left) **One of the design goals was to create distinct seating areas in the living room. This one can accommodate a small meeting or afternoon coffee hour. The area is kept light and airy with an all-white background and nearly white fabric on the couch and rug below. A subtle diamond and dot pattern works its way from the fabric into the rug pattern.**

float up the staircase. Not only did this lighten the entry-way but also it created a conversation piece for guests; when the front door opens, the feathers all puff out and, as they rise and fall, guests can't help but smile!

To accommodate small meetings with friends, the living room is arranged in three distinct seating areas. Replacing some books on the shelves with photos opened up the views and lightened the room. Three small wall sconces with wood bases have a nice relationship with the wood floor beneath. The fabric on the couch, a little repeating diamond and dot pattern, matches the custom rug that it sits on, except the dark and light tones are in reverse. The effect is a seamless, simple view; the rug looks like it is turning into the fabric. The French side chair is covered in a blush-pink taffeta fabric that extends the dash of color to the couch. The little pedestal side table is perfect for taking notes or coffee for three.

(opposite) **Here, the view into a quiet little corner is woven with differing design periods. But, with Noriega-Ortiz's wise design eye, compatibility reigns and interest is perked. He does not over-ornament; instead he allows each piece plenty of space so every feature can be fully appreciated.**

(following pages, left) **The designer kept the theme open and clean in the dining room. The rich wood furnishings stand out against the subtle, soft color scheme. The translucent window shades filter the sun, while keeping the room open to the outdoor views. The button back fabric shells on the chairs hold the look and add a touch of elegance.**

(following pages, right) **When the front door opens, the ostrich feathers on this lampshade move in the breeze as if in flight. Sitting on a cloud of white metallic silk and a feather-patterned rug, the lamp creates a pleasing view from any angle.**

Photos: Peter Margonelli

glass box rejuvenation

When New York designer Eric Cohler first came to see this home, it was in a sorry state. It had been badly damaged in a fire and little was left of the creation attributed to

Eric Cohler

renowned designer Marcel Breuer, contemporary of Philip Johnson. The once chic glass box built in the woods of Litchfield, Connecticut, in the mid-1900s was being practically given away. But it captured Cohler's imagination, and he took on the grand project of restoring, rebuilding, adding to, and personalizing the space.

Built into the side of a hill, the house opens onto a big cantilevered terrace that overlooks a trout stream complete with little rapids and lots of local wildlife. The house was aptly named Turkey Run, as hundreds of wild turkeys share the property with owls, deer, and cranes. Wings or "little buildings" were added to the glass box to create a series of linked pavilions. However, to keep the integrity of the glass box and link it to its 1960s roots, the birch plywood paneling of pre-fire days was restored. The new wings are lined in sheetrock with simple, clean moldings. Natural birch floors show their knots and give the space a sense of light.

Even more light is brought into the space through six over-sized skylights and walls of glass. The glass is the kind used in office buildings and has a bronze tint that helps keep the space cool in summer. Original Greek revival and Colonial elements were salvaged from local houses and incorporated in the design. The wings are connected to the glass box with a double-height entry—Cohler's version of a Tuscan tower. "The whole house is about being inside and outside, and about transparency—looking from one room to another," he says.

The mix of furnishings, fabric, and art is in keeping with the casual and comfortable mood. Names like Hinson, Brunschwig & Fils, Clarence House, John Saladino, and even Crate and Barrel are familiar to this home's design resume. The glass-topped, steel-legged dining room table, for example, is from Crate and Barrel, and it is surrounded by six 1820s Regency chairs from London. Covered in a creamy linen fabric from Dunghia, the seats almost disappear into the birch floor below. The ends of the table are anchored by totally different, sleek, black-armed chairs by Mies van der Rohe. Notice how the table seems to float in the room, allowing the outdoor view to remain the focus.

Although the design goal was to bring the house back to its roots, it stops short with respect to the muted palette. The taupe, beige, and milky cream are meant to subordinate the interior to the outside views and color scheme. The final creation is a series of chic glass boxes peering to, and through, the forest canopy.

(opposite) **The bedroom furniture is a mix of antique period pieces overlooked by a big, serene modern painting by Larry Charles. The green and blue is peaceful and provides a pleasant "view." The antiques, from the 1840 American Empire bed and bureau to the 1780 English Georgian chair, add rich color and depth to the room. The little Caucasian rug, circa 1860, warms up the space and suggests a seating area.**

(above) **Cohler kept the dining room simple and light, channeling the focus out-doors. The glass-topped, steel-legged table from Crate and Barrel maintains the mood and the 1820 Regency chairs from London work well with the woodsy view. The black end chairs by Mies van der Rohe quietly cap the table.**

(right) **The living room, paneled in a buttery birch, takes on a warm glow and, in combination with the views and natural light, is an irresistible place to cozy up. To further accommodate the urge to relax, a comfortable range of seating options was selected, including a cushy couch, a circa 1780 library chair properly postured for reading, and a side chair which is the perfect perch for a chat. A pretty 1945 mirrored Grosvenor House table is a good spot for afternoon tea.**

(following pages) **While guests relax by the fireplace and chat, Cohler can prepare dinner in the open kitchen, off to the right. An overscaled Chippendale-style table houses the sink and can be used for food preparation. The rebuilt fireplace is framed in local stone; a Federal mantel, circa 1810, is a perfect fit. Notice the interesting art mix on and above the mantel—everything from African masks to an 1830s American portrait.**

Photos: © Bill Geddes, 1999

The owners of this tall, narrow, 15.5-foot(4.7 meter)-wide, New York townhouse wanted Heather Faulding to make a few changes to their living space. First, the word narrow had to leave the description of their home;

F2 Inc.

grand and spacious were the new adjectives—and objectives. Second, they wanted lots and lots of storage, customized for the different needs on each floor. Third, the space had to be soundproof.

A 25-foot(7.6 meter) windowed addition to the back of the house opened the space up, as did a central staircase with open risers, lit naturally from a skylight. The lower levels include the kitchen, breakfast room, and laundry; the living room and dining room are on the next level, and the bedrooms follow above. The top floor, the most private, comprises the master bedroom and bath.

Each floor is meticulously customized to the family's taste and requirements. For example, the goal in the kitchen was to create a functional, neat room that did not feel sterile. A warm wood contrasted with stainless steel, plus a cool marble floor for texture, addressed this aim. For neatness, a rolltop, adapted from a rolltop desk design, closes off countertop cooking equipment. An ingenious bottomless cabinet above the sink allows dishes to drain without being seen, which obviates the need for a drainboard. Escape holes with sliding covers were installed at countertop, one for garbage and one for recyclables.

To accommodate one owner, a pianist who spends his day practicing, the piano was placed in a sunny corner of the living room with a garden view. Sleek, custom screens behind the piano bench circulate fresh air without allowing in mosquitoes. The dining room features a work-in-progress, glass-topped table that will eventually be held up with a fork, knife, and spoon sculpture. What looks like a wood countertop to the right of the table is really a custom bar with an icemaker, refrigerator, and drawers for wine storage; the drawers make it easier to see the bottles. The unique surface of the fireplace comes from handmade tiles baked with silver and bronze foil. Little squares of mirror climb the sides for a "dance of light."

The master bedroom, decorated in soothing lilac and silvery color tones, features lots of built-ins to address the storage requirement. The bedside tables, for example, have organizing drawers for pills and glasses, and a tray slides out for breakfast in bed. The back of the bed pulls forward for more storage; drawers set in the wall, as well as dressing rooms, expand storage capacity. Also on the master level, a study is furnished complete with a napping couch. Metal behind sheetrock walls makes an instant, clean magnetic bulletin board.

(opposite) **Open to the light from the central staircase, the unique master bath vanity feels both airy and private in this top-floor perch. The brushed silver, marble, and glass-block design elements have a clean Art Deco feel. The bathroom is behind one door and a shower behind the other. The couple enjoys a "huge blast" of sunlight in the morning.**

(above) **The placement of the grand piano in the windowed corner suits the pianist, who works here all day. The light, trees, and fresh air provide a pleasant workspace and give a new dimension to the room. Prior to the addition of twenty-five feet (7.6 meters) at the back, the house was dark and sorely lacking in living and storage space.**

(right) **The dining room's work-in-progress, glass-topped table will eventually be held up with a fork, knife and spoon sculpture. The shimmering silver fireplace surface comes from handmade tiles that have been baked with both silver and bronze foil, the creation of palm springs artist Ramona Rowley. Little squares of mirror climb the sides for a "dance of light." The oil painting that depicts New York City's Grand Central Station at rush hour makes for a wonderful background in this otherwise peaceful looking place. Called "steps grand central," it is the last in a series on the famous train station by artist Bill Jacklin.**

Photos: Stuart O'Sullivan

at home in the land

John Silverio

Located on one hundred acres (40 hectares) along the Atlantic coast, this casual Maine house sits among ferns and spruce in a micro-compound that includes a farmhouse, a cabin, and an eighteenth-century Cape Cod-style house, all now vacation rentals. The concept was to maintain the integrity of the land, keep open space clear, and respect the local wildlife that has called this area home for a long time. Land conservation planner Jerry Bley was consulted before the final site was chosen. Built for a woman who summered on this land as a youngster, this sprawling shingled cottage brings together views that she wanted in her life forever. Local architect John Silverio's assignment was to create a comfortable, sturdy home where the owner could work, entertain, and live simply.

The first floor is quite open, with an abundance of windows, doors, and decks that hug the outdoors. Two-over-two windows keep the views clean and big. Silverio made an exception to the design when he built the big two-over-two window in the living room with an arched top marking the center of the room. And it is here in the living room that most of day-to-day activities take place, all purposely sited to play off the sun's cycles. The master bedroom faces east for sunrise and the kitchen enjoys a sunset view during dinner preparations.

(right) **Set up, ready for a summer evening dinner, this seaside porch on the shoreline of Maine seems to ask, "What more do we need in life?" One can almost smell the fresh air and hear the lapping of water at the foot of the hill. In winter, with snow blanketing the green and snaking along the tree branches, the spirit is equally intoxicating.**

In the kitchen, the beadboard walls, open cabinets, and stainless-steel countertops give a hardworking look to the kitchen, which the owner wanted. Off to the right is a little workroom with a potting sink; this room also functions as dog headquarters. A vegetable and flower garden are conveniently located just outside the kitchen. The cool green woodwork sits quietly in the background, letting the kitchen views and natural light take over. A simple wooden table that serves as a lunch spot for two becomes a worktable when the owner cooks for a crowd.

Steps from the kitchen is an enchanting porch—with full, open views down to the shore—that functions as a dining room in the summer; in winter the table is moved in closer to the kitchen and the porch is used as a sunroom. Sliding glass doors shut out the cold and keep the views of Mussel Ridge clear. Also on the water side is the living room, which can accommodate two seating groups—one in front the arched window and the other by the fireplace. Depending on the light of day or the season, guests can choose to sit in the morning sunshine by the window, on the porch, on the deck, or beside the fireplace.

Furnishings are simple and casual, and seating areas have slipcovers to maintain the mood. The primary heating system is a radiant concrete slab fed by a gas boiler. Scored with a tile pattern, stained green, and waxed to a patina, it covers all of the floors and sits back in the design scheme. An alternative heating source is a Finnish-style masonry heater built by Pat Manley of Brick Stove Works in Washington, Maine; when the doors are open it works just like any other fireplace, but with the doors closed the unit heats the entire first floor. The second floor of the house comprises a guest bedroom and the owner's office and studio.

(opposite) **Morning sunshine makes this a great spot to sit and read or chat. Notice how the furnishings are all about function rather than fashion. The two couches invite one to sit, and their clean lines and twin views simply say, "Enjoy." There is nothing showy here; the needlepoint dog pillows depict favored family members.**

(following pages) **The open floor plan brings natural light pouring into the house and exposes panoramic seaside views. Screen doors that lead to balconies and the lawn provide plenty of ways to escape to the outdoors. Seating choices include the cozy sofa near the fireplace and the comfortable furniture on the porch. Furnishings are simple and functional; many are the creations of the owner's friends. The little wooden table in front of the fireplace is made from wood found on the beach. Fresh flowers add color and vivify corners.**

Photos: Brian Vanden Brink

graphic details

The annual ritual for the couple who owns this New York summer house is to arrive Memorial Day, lift the sheets off all the furnishings, and settle down for three months of rest, relaxation, and lots of entertaining.

Glen Gissler

But one frigid winter night after the water pipes burst, this getaway was devastated, and interior designer Glenn Gissler was put in charge of the major and much-needed facelift. As this is a summer home, but not part of a beach community, Gissler felt it was important to find a design balance between formality and informality, one he characterizes as an "easy formality." This was accomplished by keeping a simple color palette, and using natural materials for area floor covers (sea grass and cotton rugs), relaxed linen curtains, and furnishings that combine the rustic with the fine.

The space has a plantation-like quality; the design subtly recalls this with the introduction of dark wood furnishings, a mix of new and antique pieces, and a grand scale created with an open living room layout. "Moments of green," expressed in details like a pillow, vase, palm tree, or fabric-covered footstool, add just enough color but maintain the visual calm. This styling also makes it easy for the owners to have the room look right; there's not a lot to worry about or readjust when company comes or goes.

(right) **The design goal was a mood of "easy formality" that would play up the plantation feel which suggested itself here. This was achieved with a neutral palette, an open furnishing layout, and the introduction of rich, dark woods that give the room a graphic quality.**

Nothing here is too precious, fancy, or pretentious, and by not over-furnishing, what is here "reads distinctly and has a graphic quality." Notice the little footstool, an example of the nineteenth-century American aesthetic movement, opposite the white tufted chair and the William Morris Liberty chair with the rush seat.

Also, keeping all upholstery neutral gives the dark woods clarity and punch, and spotlights all of the interesting objects integrated in the room. The living room's bare wood folding screen turns an empty corner into a place of visual interest and creates pleasing shadows across the floor in the afternoon sun. The mahogany pedestal table in front of the screen and the nearby lamp share a wooden barley twist on their bases as a distinguishing detail. The wood floors were stained dark to keep the room crisp.

To accommodate parties, a custom mahogany dining room table can expand to seat fourteen. The cane-seated wooden chairs—Anglo-Indian style—represent the perfect balance of formality, informality, and style. Antique steel lamps from England light the table; a floor lamp brightens conversation as well as a corner. The teardrop silk lampshade is an hand-painted creation of Mariano Fortuny. The custom-made, beveled-edge mirror reflects the rich reds of the table and chairs as well as a nineteenth-century Chinese herb chest that hangs on the opposite wall.

Gissler designed a sleek storage area below the mirror which is topped with honed stone that maintains a graphic quality. Shuttered windows, a wooden ceiling fan, and an antique-style iron bed carry the plantation feeling through to the bedroom. The details of the antique bed and painted trunk stand out opposite the stark white bed linens.

(opposite) **The master bedroom carries the plantation feel with its wooden ceiling fan, shuttered windows, and antique-style iron bed. A pair of cotton, checked rugs in green and white are set over the dark stained hardwood floor. And, as in other rooms, choice antique pieces complete the design.**

(above) **Nothing here is too precious. If more seating is needed, the Tibetan trunk—usually serving as a coffee table—can be used. With the exception of few chairs, furnishings are slipcovered for easy cleaning.**

(opposite) **To accommodate dinner for fourteen, Gissler designed this big, wide mahogany table and chose casual Anglo-Indian cane chairs to frame it. The antique steel lamps are from England and add another casual touch to the decor.**

Photos: John Hall

Once, this elegant, clubby room served as the reception area in a turn-of-the-century Manhattan townhouse. It was, according to designer James Rixner, the place where the

James Rixner

host and hostess greeted guests before directing them into the library. In the 1930s, the home was turned into elegant one-room apartments, and transition areas like the landing became small bathrooms and kitchens. When Kips Bay took over the building, all renovations were removed, and Rixner, like others, had a clean slate to work with. The step back in time sought by the designer was meant to create a room "caught in a perpetual cocktail hour." The inspiration for the styling originated in two French steamer chairs found at the shop of a local antique dealer, Alan Moss.

A fireplace was selected to be the focus of the room, with all activity clustered around it. But this is no ordinary fireplace; it is a magnificent vertical art object made of inlaid zebrawood. The wood was commonly used in the 1920s, but it was often sealed, becoming darker and more solemn. This approach retains the light honey shade by means of an amber glaze. The fireplace is designed to accentuate the vertical lines of the room. The 10-foot (3-meter) ceilings play well against the stripes, and the band of horizontal zebrawood that tops it off helps to push the walls out and the ceiling up. Zebrawood is also used as a base to display the sculpture. A light box of the same, built at ceiling height, sends light washing down the wall to illuminate the art below.

A simple, but unusual palette of pistachio, copper, and gold sweeps across the room. It begins with the hand-tinted ceiling papered with a square motif, moves to the upholstery, and continues down to the custom Sisel wool rug, where one of every four squares is pistachio. The square motif recurs on all of the iridescent silk fabric—a new line called Fadini from Boussac—except the walls, which are upholstered in pistachio silk.

The arresting male and female sculptures on either side of the fireplace are hand-cast plaster. They were created by Hilarie Johnston as a commission by Rixner. They work well with the vertical thrust of the wood pattern. *The Bathers,* the Alexandre Iacovleff painting behind the couch, is a fabulous addition to this serene room and links well visually

(opposite) **Rixner commissioned the ceiling lamp from Brooklyn artist Joseph Pagano. The glass is tinted pistachio and copper; ornate antique fittings pull the look together. Completing the feeling in the room is *The Bathers,* a 1929 oil painting by Alexandre Iacovleff.**

(right) **Designer James Rixner wanted people who step into this room to feel caught in a "perpetual cocktail hour," to catch its mood of relaxed elegance. The simple, unusual color palette contributes to this goal, as does the floor-to-ceiling square motif, reflected in the nubby silk upholstery and the vintage French furnishings. The inspiration for the room's styling came from the pair of rare Eugene Printz steamer chairs, which reflect the design of Jean-Michel Frank.**

Photos: Bill Rothschild

Jacob D. Albert
Albert, Righter, Tittman Architects, Inc.
58 Winter Street
Boston, MA 02108
phone: 617.451.5740
fax: 617.451.2309
email@albertrightertittman.com

Rick Berns
Berns Fry Interiors
75 Swamp Road
East Hampton, NY 11937
212.388.1700

Jeffery Bilhuber
330 East 59th Street, 6th Floor
New York, NY 10022
phone: 212.308.4888
fax: 212.223.4590
bilhuber@aol.com

Lee Bogart
Lee Bogart Interior Design
250 Birch Hill Road
Locust Valley
Long Island, NY 11560
phone: 516.676.3881

Laura Bohn
Laura Bohn Design Associates
30 West 26th Street
New York, NY 10010
phone: 212.645.3636
fax: 212.645.3639

R. Scott Bromley
Bromley-Caldari Architects PC
242 West 27th Street
New York, NY 10001
phone: 212.620.4250

Linda Chase
Linda Chase Associates Inc.
482 Town Street
East Haddam, CT 06423
phone: 860.873.9499
fax: 860.873.9496

Eric Cohler
17 East 96th Street
New York, NY 10128
phone: 212.876.1518
fax: 212.876.8393

Christopher Coleman
70 Washington Street, Suite 1105
Brooklyn, NY 11201
phone: 718.222.8984
fax: 718.222.8983

Celeste Cooper
1415 Boylston Street
Boston, MA 02116
phone: 212.826.5667
fax: 617.426.1879

Mary Douglas Drysdale
Drysdale Design, Inc.
1733 Connecticut Avenue, NW
Washington, DC 20009.
phone: 202.588.0700

Matt Elliott
Elliott & Elliott Architects
P. O. Box 318
Blue Hill, ME 04614
phone: 207.374.2566
fax: 207.374.2567
elliott@acadia.net

Heather Faulding
F2 Inc. & Faulding Associates
11 East 22nd Street
New York, NY 10010
phone: 212.253.1513

Peter Forbes
Peter Forbes & Associates
70 Long Wharf
Boston, MA 02110
phone: 617.523.5800
fax: 617.523.5810
forbes@psa.bos.com

Michael Gabellini
Gabellini Associates Architects
665 Broadway
New York, NY 10012
phone: 212.388.1700

Glenn Gissler
Glenn Gissler Design Inc.
36 East 22nd Street, 8th Floor
New York, NY 10010-6124
phone: 212.228.9880

Zina Glazebrook
Z.G. Designs
10 Wireless Road
East Hampton, NY 11937
phone: 519.329.7486

Albert Hadley
Parish Hadley Associates, Inc.
24 East 64st Street
New York, NY 10021
phone: 212.888.7979
fax: 212.888.5597

Dakota Jackson
Dakota Jackson, Inc.
42-24 Orchard Street, 5th Floor
Long Island City, NY 11101
phone: 718.786.8600

Thomas Jayne
Thomas Jayne Studio, Inc.
136 East 57th Street, Room 1304
New York, NY 10022
phone: 212.838.9080
fax: 212.838.9654

Lynn Morgan
19 Hilltop Road, Wilson Point
South Norwalk, CT 06854
phone: 203.854.5037

Reed Morrison
Reed Morrison Associates
193 Parker Road
Osterville, MA 02655
phone: 508.428.8379

Benjamin Noriega-Ortiz
75 Spring Street
New York, NY 10012
phone: 212.343.9363

Thomas O'Brien
132 Spring Street
New York, NY 10012
phone: 212.966.4700
fax: 212.966.4701

Jennifer Post
25 East 67th Street
New York, NY 10021
phone: 212.734.7994
fax: 212.936.2450

James Rixner
121 Morton Street, #4B
New York, NY 10014
phone: 212.206.7439
fax: 212.206.6636

Winton Scott
Winton Scott Architects
5 Milk Street
Portland, ME 04101
phone: 207.774.4811
fax: 207.774.3083

Peter Shelton
Lee Mindel
Shelton Mindel Associates
216 West 18th Street
New York, NY 10011
phone: 212.243.3939
fax: 212.727.7310

John Silverio
RR1 Box 4725
Lincolnville, ME 04849
phone: 207.763.4652

William Sofield
Studio Sofield Inc.
380 Lafayette Street
New York, NY 1000
phone: 212.473.1300

Charles Spada
1 Design Center Place
Boston, MA 02210
phone: 617.951.0008
fax: 617.951.9900

Vicente Wolf
333 West 39th Street, 10th Floor
New York, NY 10018
phone: 212.465.0590
fax: 212.465.0639

Andrew Bordwin
Andrew Bordwin Studio, Inc.
70A Greenwich Avenue
New York, NY 10011
phone: 212.627.9519
fax: 212.924.1791

John Coolidge
425 W. 24th Street, #4A
New York, NY 10011
phone: 212.581.0181

Michael Dunne
54 Stokenchurch Street
London SW6 3TR
England
phone: 44.171.736.617
fax: 44.171.731.8794

Pieter Estersohn
Pieter Estersohn Photography
c/o La Chapelle Representation Ltd.
420 E. 54th Street
New York, NY 10022
phone: 212.838.3170
fax: 212.758.6199

Andrew Garn
85 East 10th Street
New York, NY 10003
phone: 212.353.8434
fax: 212.353.8434

Bill Geddes
Bill Geddes Photographer
215 West 78th Street
New York, NY 10024
phone: 212.799.4464
fax: 212.799.5576

John M. Hall
John M. Hall Photography
500 West 58th Street, 3F
New York, NY 10019
phone: 212.757.0369

Andrew Lautman
Lautman Photography
4906 41st Street NW
Washington, D. C. 20011
phone: 202.966.2800
fax: 202.966.4240

Richard S. Mandelkorn
RSM Photography
65 Beaver Pond Road
Lincoln, MA 01773
phone: 781.259.3310
fax: 781.259.3312

Peter Margonelli
20 Desbrosses Street
New York, NY 10013-1704
phone: 212.941.0380

Michael Moran
Michael Moran Photography, Inc.
371 Broadway, 2nd Floor
New York, NY 10013
phone: 212.334.4543
fax: 212.334.3854

Michael Mundy
Michael Mundy Photographer Inc.
25 Mercer Street, #3B
New York, NY 10013
phone: 212.226.4741
fax: 212.343.2936

Sam Ogden
Sam Ogden Photography
273 Summer Street
Boston, MA 02210
phone: 617.426.1021
fax: 617.426.1021

Stuart O'Sullivan
29 Clinton Street, #10
New York, NY 10002
phone: 212.677.4509

David Lewis Phelps
David Phelps Photography
6305 Yucca Street, #601
Los Angeles, CA 90001
phone: 323.464.7237
fax: 323.464.7238

Laura Resen
422 West Broadway, #3
New York, NY 10012
phone: 212.334.1862
fax: 212.334.1864

Eric Roth
Eric Roth Photography
P. O. Box 422
Topsfield, MA01983
phone: 978.887.1975
fax: 978.887.5035

Bill Rothschild
19 Judith Lane
Monsey, NY 10952
phone: 212.752.3674 and
phone: 914.354.4567

James R. Salomon
James R. Salomon Photo, Inc.
P. O. Box 4654
Portland, ME 04112
phone: 207.767.3904
fax: 207.767.3904

Stan Schnier
66 West 88th Street
New York, NY 10024-2503
phone: 212.874.0292
fax: 212.874.7463

Brian Vanden Brink
P. O. Box 419
Rockport, ME 04856
phone: 207.236.4035.
fax: 207.236.0704

William Waldron
William Waldron Photography
27 Bleeker Street, 6A
New York, NY 10012

Paul Warchol
Paul Warchol Photography
224 Centre Street
New York, NY 10013
phone: 212.431.3461
fax: 212.274.1953

Nick Wheeler
c/o Peter Forbes
70 Long Wharf
Boston, MA 02110
phone: 617.523.5800
fax: 617.523.5810

about the author

Anna Kasabian has twenty-five years of experience as a
writer, editor, and communications professional. She has
written on numerous topics, including living, gardening,
dining, traveling, and antiqueing in New England, but her
greatest passion is exploring modern interiors and archi-
tecturally significant homes, inns, hotels, and gardens. She
is also the author of *Designing Interiors with Tile: Creative
Ideas with Ceramics, Stone, and Mosaic,* published by
Rockport Publishers. Her byline frequently appears in
Design Times magazine, where she writes about residen-
tial and getaway design projects, and in the *Boston Globe,*
where she writes on interior design and exploring and preserving New England mansions, gardens, and homesteads.